# Broken Chapters

21 Testimonies of How God
Rewrites Our Life Stories

Compiled by Krista Dunk, with Suzette Adao,
Heather Ferrante, Andy Bunch, Rhonda Castanon,
Susan Fujii, Liz Jack, Kari L. Jones, Judi Kruis,
DelShanna Moore, Yvonne Mutch, Eileen Noyes, Renée
Parris, Mark Pollish, Rosanne Roberts Archuletta, Joelene
Powell,
Debi Shannon, Jenny Swart, Angela Yarborough,
Desiree T. Young, and Cheryl Zalewski

**100X**
PUBLISHING

# Broken Chapters Authors:

Compiled by Krista Dunk
Suzette Adao
Heather Ferrante
Andy Bunch
Rhonda Castanon
Susan Fujii
Liz Jack
Kari L. Jones
Judi Kruis
DelShanna Moore
Yvonne Mutch
Eileen Noyes
Renée Parris
Mark Pollish
Rosanne Roberts Archuletta
Joelene Powell
Debi Shannon
Jenny Swart
Angela Yarborough
Desiree T. Young
Cheryl Zalewski

This book is dedicated to the Lord, the Master Author, and to all those who need to know He can rewrite their broken chapter too.

*For the testimony of Jesus is the spirit of prophecy.*
—Revelation 19:10b

# CONTENTS

# ABOUT THIS BOOK

In the fall of 2022, I had the God idea to gather stories from others; stories about the *Broken Chapters* of life. We all have a broken chapter or two—some short in duration and some long, from deeply disappointing to tragic. So, I put out the call to my author community and sphere of Kingdom friends. Along with writing my own story, twenty others answered the call, and this book was born.

In each chapter, the author writes about their real-life experiences and how they saw God show up in the midst of their pain. God is still in the business of restoring joy, restoring fortunes, restoring identity, and healing our broken places today. Nothing is too difficult for Him.

I want to express my gratitude to each person who was willing to share their story here. When other people share their stories of what God has done for them, we get a boost of faith. A spark is lit within us that says *if God can do it for them, He can do it for me, too.*

This is our hope and prayer for you, reader. We hope you say, "Wow, look what God has done!" And in some cases hearing or reading others' stories causes us to realize His great ability and care for the first time. *Look what God can do!* He does care about you. He does care about what you've gone through. He does care about you finding hope, finding peace, finding resolution, finding healing, and most of all, finding Him.

His eternal pen still writes and rewrites today, bringing beauty for ashes and working out all types of circumstances for good for those who love Him and are called to live according to His plans and purposes.

Thank you for reading. Now, it's time for you to be infused with faith and hope for your *Broken Chapters* to be rewritten.

—Krista Dunk, author and publisher

**Renée Parris**, Financial Strategist, Coach, Encourager

Renée Parris grew up in a small coal mining town in Kentucky. Surrounded by the Appalachian Mountains and a host of relatives, she learned early in life the value of family, friends, and faith.

Along with her husband of 37 years and two children, Renée lives in North Carolina where she owns and runs several businesses and is very involved in ministry and missions projects. Their family is passionate about encouraging other families who parent children with special needs or have experienced grief. After 17 years of infertility, multiples miscarriages, stillborn death and a premature birth, Renée and her husband have chosen to funnel their love and desire for a large family into caring for other people's children. They have fostered 38 children in their home, mentored and provided short term places of respite for teenage girls who needed a safe place to land. God has expanded their borders and allowed them to parent so many more children than if they had not lost the four children that await them in Heaven.

Professionally, Renée is a serial entrepreneur and loves business. Her primary business is as a Financial Strategist and Business Coach specializing in retirement planning and growth strategies for clients of Forecast Financial Group. LLC. She is also a founder and partner in Elite Agent Solutions, LLC where she trains and supports insurance agents and advisors. Renée draws upon her decades of corporate, entrepreneurial, and non-profit management experience to relate to clients from all walks of life and career experiences.

Financial/business email:
**renee@forecastfinancialgroup.com**
Grief/special needs parenting email:
**parrisrenee@yahoo.com**
Facebook: Renee Crawford Parris
Blog: **hearmyheartbeat.wordpress.com**

# The Journey Through Grief

Somewhere in the foggy distance, there was a familiar, guttural sound like the crying of an injured animal. As I struggled to figure out where it was coming from, slowly, my mind awoke to realize the noise was projecting from my own body. From a heart so broken by grief, I didn't know moment by moment if I had the physical strength to take the next breath. Sleep was my only escape from pain. Waking up meant the unimaginable despair would return. *Our son is gone* became the first thought my brain formed each time I awoke.

Sadly, this pain was all too familiar. I am no stranger to grief. Seventeen years of marriage had brought years of infertility, the devastating miscarriages of three little girls, and a premature birth of another precious girl born much too soon, weighing way too little and with far too many complications. She was a medical mess yet a beautiful gift to our family. And now, two years later, we were grieving once again for our dreamed of, longed for, and prayed over, full-term son, Jonathan Michael, who unexplainably died during delivery.

*How do you celebrate a birth that's preceded by death? What do you do with months of anticipation when instantly it slams into devastation? How many children do we have to say goodbye to before we said hello? How do you process holding a death certificate for someone for whom there was no birth certificate? That seems cruel.* These were my heart's questions and groanings only God could understand.

*Parenthood.* The word conjures up a host of emotions and words that we long for and dream of for years. *Planning. Expectations. Anticipation. Celebration.* Millions of women have experienced the miracle of motherhood. The transition from a woman with a whole heart into a woman with a capacity to have her heart live both inside and outside of her body is a beautiful and miraculous process. A woman's heart is never again whole once she has children; each child carries a piece of her heart with them through life, whether they live in Heaven or on earth. Our capacity for love grows with each pregnancy or adoption, as unexplainable reserves of love make their way into our hearts for each new child.

Yet, because we live in a broken world suspended between the perfection of the Garden of Eden and Heaven, we understand that life is not always carefree. Sometimes, earth-shattering events happen that shake our foundation and alter us forever.

Infertility, miscarriage, stillborn, prematurity, death—harsh, ugly words that no one wants to say much less experience as part of their journey in life. Yet, too many of us have one or more of those as part of our life's resume. Known as grief, there is a process we go through when our hearts are disappointed, when we lose people or dreams we loved and held onto in our souls.

And when children we carried beneath our breasts—those who lived and breathed, those whose hearts beat within us—leave us, part of our heart goes to Heaven with them. When we miscarry, hormones rage. The ovaries and uterus contract, trying to find their rhythm again, leaving us with unpredictable emotions. When death comes to a child, the word *sorrow* takes on a depth of unexplainable meaning. When we long for a child and fertility eludes us, empty wombs and arms seem to betray our femininity.

Grief includes waves of sadness that suffocate us, making breathing seem a difficult chore. In our valley, words spoken by well-meaning and good intentioned friends seem shallow. Maybe most painful of all is that human comfort is lost for a season, and we feel utterly alone.

How do I feel about grief? It feels a bit like God's decisions slamming into my day, altering my reality. My feelings get hurt and my heart is wounded. I love Him. I trust His sovereignty, but there are weak, fleeting moments when I am quite sure I don't agree with His choices. Until my heart heals, and grief—while never ending—does become an accepted friend, I remember God's ways are always, always higher and better than mine.

My dream was six blond-haired girls donning tiaras, frilly tutus, and dress-up clothes trying to balance themselves in Momma's high heeled shoes. Picnic baskets lined up on quilts covering the grassy carpets of the rolling hills. Daisies tied in blond hair while running through evening fields chasing fireflies. Tea parties with lace doilies and eyelet-trimmed dresses. Late night chats in floor length nightgowns, sharing secrets and dreams. Wedding gowns and bouquets on the horizon. These were my six girls, my gifts to send out into the world, my greatest accomplishments, and my cherished friends. They were and are my unfulfilled dream.

Our first three little ones lived in my body for far too short a time and then moved to the heavenly nursery which, in my estimation, is much too far away. We believed they were girls and named them Faith, Hope, and Charity. Then came our sweet Emma Grace. In our dream she would be perfect and healthy. In God's dream—our reality—she's a medical mess of a gift who shows God's love to everyone she encounters.

> **Dreaming became too painful after Jonathan, and so we stopped dreaming.**

We dared to dream once more, but again our dream was trumped. Jonathan Michael was stillborn. Dreaming became too painful after Jonathan, and so we stopped dreaming. Our home would be complete with just the three of us. *Emma is enough.* She kept us busy and we cherished the opportunity to be her parents. We pushed her hard to reach her potential and tried to give her everything we possibly could to resemble a normal life in spite of her physical limitations.

Psalm 21:2 says, "Thou hast given him his heart's desire…" In His sovereignty, God dreamed for us again. He would give us six pregnancies in total. That much of mine and His dreams aligned. But His plans would unfold in years of infertility, three miscarriages, one premature birth, one full-term stillborn death, and then one miracle birth of a son, Spencer Michael, who changed us forever and was the balm of Gilead to my soul.

What I have learned is that the best dreams are those we don't even dare to dream for ourselves. Dreams born in the heart of God within the corridors of Heaven; those are the best ones.

Often, God's dreams take a while to unravel and come to fruition. We see the stages of development and waiting as painful, uncaring, not in our best interest, or even unfair. How silly we are to doubt that the One who created us would ever dream anything for us other than what's best. I'm sad for all the times I've doubted; His dreams for me were far better than my dreams for myself.

Let me tell you about Jonathan, our stillborn son. Time is interesting, fleeting, hard to explain. Often, time seems to pass quickly. Sometimes it eeks by, and other times, it stands still.

When the doctor confirmed what our hearts already knew, that Jonathan Michael had unexpectedly and unexplainably passed away, time stood still in my soul. Suspended between the maternity suite at Duke Hospital and Heaven, my mind couldn't process that the child I had carried and who had been the answer to a decade of prayers was now gone. The minutes passed and the hours dragged on; *I don't know if time will ever matter again.*

After a tragedy, I'd heard people say they didn't want to go on; they weren't sure if they could move forward amidst their grief. I thought I could relate, but I really didn't. Even after three miscarriages and a premature delivery of Emma Grace, I had never felt despair like I did when Jonathan died. Not that I ever contemplated not living, but the pain was so intense I didn't know if my heart could physically keep on beating. It was broken in more pieces and ways than I knew was possible.

**Tears flowed until there were no more left.**

Yet, time did pass. Minutes did become hours, and days did flow into weeks. People came and loved on us. Tears flowed until there were no more left. Memories rushed in when least expected and still do. Grief sneaks up and takes me by surprise even now. A song, a white rose, the pattern of blue gingham material, yellow rubber duckies, every time I walk into Duke Hospital—oh so many triggers take me back to the moment when our precious boy found himself in the arms of Jesus instead of my arms where I thought he belonged.

Specifically, when I remember Jonathan, I realize how blessed I am for having shared nine beautiful months with him. It is not lost on me that I'm the only human being to have felt him move or know what it felt like when he had the hiccups. I was the one who could sing to him and know he was reacting to my voice. I was the one who first held him once he was delivered from the safety of my womb and the last to touch his precious face before the casket—that became his crib instead of the one I had decorated for him—was closed.

I remember every detail of him—his tiny body was perfect. Long, adorable fingers and toes, wispy blond hair, soft newborn skin, and the most beautiful, round face that's etched deeply in my mind and heart. But inside that precious, small body was a heart that wasn't beating as it had been just hours before, beneath my own heart.

I remember that day and the days that followed. The 48 long, grueling hours of labor to deliver him, the dozens of details involved in planning a funeral to be as perfect as he was, the physical trauma and healing process following his birth, the days of moving into a home that was supposed to include a beautiful nursery but instead held an empty bedroom.

Even now I remember the weight of him in my arms. How wonderful it felt to cradle his precious, yet still, body even for those brief moments. He is really just a heartbeat away, and he began his earthly life beneath my heart which he continues to occupy a huge space in today.

He was ours. God hand selected me to be his mother and Mike to be his father. Of all the parents in the world, He graced us with that privilege. How blessed we are.

Still with each birthday, I cry and remember and wish he was here. How I wish he could blow out candles on his birthday cake, unwrap presents, celebrate with friends, and know how very much he is loved.

Someone asked me a strange question once: if time could be turned back and I could choose, would I have chosen to never have conceived Jonathan or have been pregnant and suffered the loss? A thousand times over I would do every single second of that pregnancy again. To have known of the wonder and secrecy of him before the news was shared with the world. To have felt him moving beneath my heart and know he was growing and thriving in the most sacred place inside my womb. To have dreamed and enjoyed imagining him for all of those months. And to have held him in my arms for those very brief hours. Yes, a thousand times over...*YES.*

God's grace truly is amazing. His comfort and peace are unexplainable. His tenderness in meeting me in the deepest ravines of grief and whispering His love when I could not hear any other voices around me sustained me. He came deep down into the valley, blew life into me again, resuscitated my broken heart, and held my hand as I slowly, oh so slowly, climbed out of the depths and back into a new normal.

Sometimes when I think of all that our children in Heaven have missed out on here, living everyday life with us, my eyes fill with tears and my heart physically hurts. There were so many things I wanted to show them, teach them, and experience with them. So many amazing people we call family and friends who they would have enjoyed. And if God had given me a choice, of course, I would have chosen to keep them here. Yet, I am also grateful for what they've missed. They've never had to know sickness, loneliness, pain, or tears. Those are things they have been shielded from because of the sovereignty of God.

Years have come and gone since each of our losses. One day after another has continuously flowed. And we know, on this side of Heaven, there will be more loss. Oh, but isn't the Lord amazing? He had a plan to patch up my heart. He had a wonderful way of healing the gaping wound I thought would be wide open forever. God is altogether lovely and amazing. He allowed me to carry six children and was gracious enough to allow two of those children to survive. Infertility, miscarriage, prematurity, and loss are woven into the patchwork quilt of parenthood for us. Yet so are the lives of Emma Grace and Spencer Michael; they have added their own beautiful designs to the quilt of our lives. We are truly blessed.

When it comes to grief, it may be one of the most difficult experiences to translate into words. It affects each person differently and is no respecter of time. Whenever grief sneaks up on us, it's as raw as the moment it first showed up. Some have tried to break it down into phases or stages to help us understand its power.

The stages of grief are filled with days when it's hard to imagine if *this too shall pass* will ever be accurate—days when it's easier to stay under the covers than to get up and face the world. Sometimes grief hits us so hard that the very act of breathing becomes difficult. Each breath strains against the muscles to take in and release air. *Will I survive the next moment?* Thinking beyond the instant feels impossible.

> **Sometimes grief hits us so hard that the very act of breathing becomes difficult.**

Although it's not a badge of honor I would have sought after, I can say that I'm well acquainted with grief. It has been my companion more times than I would have chosen. Ironically, it has also been my friend and the one tool God has used more than any other to shape me, refine me, challenge me, and use me.

My first experience with grief was at the young age of seven. On July 4, Independence Day, my grandfather passed away from cancer and black lung disease. I'm not sure how much we can truly understand about death at that age, but I do remember the pain of grieving. Up to that point in my life, it was the deepest despair I had known. I can still recall the pain I felt and how desperately I just wanted to be held.

How many times since that July 4th summer day have I come to God grieving, broken, carrying pieces of shattered dreams, bearing open wounds, and sobbing tears that took away the ability to speak? Often! Whenever and wherever death is present, there is freedom to grieve with God. He will hold us as long as we need to be held—until our tears dry and we feel like we can inhale deeply, filling our lungs with physical air and spiritual strength enough to stand on our own again. I just love that about Him.

When just one small moment in life shatters our perfect day and everything we knew as good is gone, God's arms cocoon us in an embrace. Nestled up against Him we can just sit and be still until we finally hear Him say, "In the midst of the pain, know that I'm here and everything's going to be okay." *Because You're with me, God, I will survive this.*

Grief does not always come from physical death. It could be from the loss of health, the death of a dream, a void in our heart, a diagnosis that sets us on a course of unpredictable outcomes, a betrayal that shakes our foundation of trust, or other losses that empty our daily life of companionship, ability, or well-being.

No one wants to hear bad news. We humans don't like suffering or the fears that accompany suffering. But if I know anything, God is sovereign. If I didn't believe that to my very core, I would not have survived to write this story.

No one chooses the path of grief, but when we find ourselves on it, the only hope is to move through the process and not get stuck. If we move through the stages, we can come to the end and find ourselves healed, although maybe not "whole." There is still something missing. If we get stuck in denial, anger, bitterness, etc., we live a miserable life, blaming God and wondering what happened to our plans and dreams.

When those grief moments show up in my life, I know for sure that God is already there. And that knowledge sustains me. God gives "peace that passeth all understanding" and "grace that is sufficient" when we need it most. It cannot be explained…it just is! Psalm 142:3 says, "When my spirit was overwhelmed within me, then thou knewest my path." He knows what we will face before we face it. He has ordered our steps and has a plan already laid out.

The devil is skilled at making us feel isolated and magnifying our issues to the point where we can become self-absorbed and even bitter at the very God who created us, loves us, died to redeem us, and is waiting on the other side of the beautiful clouds for us. In my own life, I've had so many opportunities to question God, but every time I've gone through a valley, I look back and see how His hand was leading and how the valley was used to strengthen me. Our three miscarriages were tough, emotionally, on our marriage. And Emma's birth and health challenges have rocked us to the core. But losing and burying our precious son Jonathan took me further into the depths of despair than anything. There were many days when I wondered if I'd survive, but I did and you will survive grief, too!

Yes, it will hurt, it will be scary, it will rock your world and challenge you in every way possible, but it's a piece of the puzzle God has crafted just for you. No one else can walk it but you. When life finds you reeling from unexpected news or just the overwhelm of life, know that God is in control and loves you so much more than you can imagine. His ways are higher than ours. The next breath may be painful, but it will come.

Grief is real; it's a painful, life-altering process. But it does not have to define us. Grief does not have to overshadow everything else good and wonderful in our lives. It is painful, intense, hard, difficult, and sometimes feels unsurvivable. I understand this completely. But God is bigger than grief. His mercies are new every morning (Lamentations 3:22-23) and His grace is abundant and sufficient (II Corinthians 12:9). If you feel stuck in the grief process, please know there is help available. Seek out godly counsel and ask God to help you move through the stages of grief so your legacy will not be defined by that one traumatic experience.

> **Grief does not have to overshadow everything else good and wonderful in our lives.**

I don't know what healing looks like for you. I don't know how God will show up and turn your ashes into beauty. I only know that He will. He is good and He has plans for us beyond our comprehension.

So, breathe deeply, my friend. You are stronger than your trial. You are not defined by grief. You will be better because of the times when grief has been your companion. God can take some pretty awful situations and mold them into beautiful places in our lives. His studio specializes in restoration of broken and damaged canvases. He meticulously restores to usefulness what others would throw away. And the work He has begun in you? Oh, He will finish it, and it will be a masterpiece. Just you wait and see.

**Suzette Adao,**
hospitality expert, co-
founder of 100X Academy

Suzette Adao is Co-Founder of 100X, the number one community and training for Kingdom entrepreneurs, and the Creator of 100X NextGen. As a devoted mother of three and the spiritual mamma of the world-wide 100X Movement, Suzette is passionate about helping others achieve their goals and live fulfilling lives. Alongside her husband Pedro, Suzette has an extensive background in real estate and entrepreneurial ventures. In addition to her professional achievements, Suzette is most renowned for her gift of hospitality, love of cooking, and generous spirit. Whether she is entertaining guests in her home or hosting large events, Suzette always goes the extra mile to ensure everyone feels welcomed and comfortable. Her caring and giving nature has earned her a special place in the hearts of those who know her.

Learn more about the 100X Movement at:

**www.100XTraining.com**

# Lay It Down on the Altar

As I was signing the receipt for my transaction, I instantly felt alive, special, and seen. But that was just for a fleeting moment. For the rest of my day, I struggled with sadness, loneliness, poor self-esteem, and lack of identity.

I know this is a very strange beginning, but let me take you back. At this point of my life, I was around 33 years old, married, and was a mother of three young children. My days were long, filled with helping my husband with the family business, busing kids to and from school, volunteering at the school, sports and cheer activities, making dinner, shopping and cleaning for a family of five, trying to stay connected with extended family, and so much more. When I look back on those days, I remember and treasure so many memories, but I also look back at who I was: an empty shell, surviving, living day by day.

There were days when the only things I looked forward to were my morning coffee, going to bed, and when I had to sign a receipt. I know, this sounds so strange. Why would signing a receipt have me excited? It was because of the compliments I was getting…about my stunning wedding ring. Nine out of ten times I would get complimented about how beautiful it was. Usually it was women noticing, but occasionally men would, too.

The more compliments I got, the more I would extend my hand out to *make sure* people would notice it. This would happen at Starbucks, grocery stores, department stores, the post office, anywhere I'd be making a transaction with money or signing something. I would make sure my hand was positioned in such a way as to *guarantee* the person helping me would see it. This was something I looked forward to in my day. I would literally look for opportunities to get a compliment from a complete stranger to make me feel special. It gave me a brief moment of fulfillment.

Let me tell you a little bit about this ring. It wasn't the ring that my husband Pedro—of now 25 years—proposed with. It was a ring that I had upgraded at least three times over the years. As we became more successful in business, going to the Jewelry Mart in San Francisco was something I liked to do. I couldn't wait to make my ring larger, grander, and with more sparkles in every way possible. Unfortunately, I did not have a connection with these upgraded rings; they had no sentimental value to me. This new ring was just a big shiny rock. Don't get me wrong, I absolutely loved it (as you can tell). It was beautiful and unique.

But the thing is, I prioritized and valued that ring because of its beauty and uniqueness, and because of that, it's where I was finding my value. *My ring is valuable and people notice it, so that makes me valuable.* I know it's silly, and you might wonder why I put such a high value on a ring and no value on myself. But at the time I felt frumpy. I felt like I had nothing to offer. I felt like I was just a mom getting by, day by day. *Nothing special.*

When I look back, I would say that I *thought* I had a good relationship with the Lord. We, as a family, would go to church every Wednesday and Sunday to worship

> **I thought I had a good relationship with the Lord.**

and fellowship, and we had some great relationships through the church. On the outside it all looked perfect—I looked perfect—but inside I was hurting. I didn't know I was searching for identity, purpose, value. I would soon to find out I *was* searching, and soon after, the Lord revealed Himself to me. But before I share that experience, I want to give you more backstory.

One of my favorite Bible verses is Jeremiah 29:11 which says, "'I know the thoughts I have toward you,' declares the Lord, 'plans to prosper you and not to harm you, to give you hope and a future.'" As a young believer, this was one of the first verses I memorized. I remember buying every picture frame, desk weight, bookmark, magnet, anything with this verse on it. This verse gave me a glimpse of hope; hope that *one day things will change for me.* Jeremiah 29:11 was something I could always hold onto, no matter what circumstances I faced. Deep down, I felt like at least I had this verse as an anchor.

But in my twenties as a new believer, I was having a hard time with my purpose. At church, they talked about our "purpose" and "identity" a lot. *How do I find these?* In my mind, I was *just a mom, just Pedro Adao's wife.* In fact, for a long time that's how I would introduce myself. "Hi, I'm Pedro's wife." God never gave me a flashing sign about what my purpose was. I was searching for a grand thing of some kind, but for that season, my purpose *was* being a mom and a wife and I didn't understand it. So, I searched.

When it came to my identity, I couldn't seem to center myself on something. Already acting in my purpose but not realizing it, I watched Pedro in a purposeful season. He was doing well in business, was in the Word often, served on the worship team, etc. Then, there was me: *just* a mom, *just* a wife. So, I started attaching myself to his identity because I couldn't recognize my own. *Pedro's wife. If I can't find my own, I'll just attach my identity to my husband.*

That was a problematic phase for me of searching desperately, yet not being able to find it. That's why I thought the ring brought identity. Looking back, I know I *was* doing something very purposeful. God put me in a season of being a caretaker of young, impressionable, precious people who needed me. Still, I was the person feeling numb, going to church, looking fine on the outside, and shriveling on the inside.

In my early thirties, we were doing financially well and keeping up with the Joneses. Even so, there were some signs of financial stress; there was a tension when it came to our business. Things weren't looking the best, and we starting to feel a shift. It wasn't flowing like it had been, but for the most part, we ignored it and pushed on.

One Wednesday night, I walked into a church service late after dropping my daughter Sofia off at her cheer practice. Pedro was already there, as he was serving on the worship team that night. While in my seat during the pastor's message, something shocking happened. Out of the blue, God spoke to me. He said, "Take off your

**"Take off your ring and leave it at the altar."**

ring and leave it at the altar." I couldn't believe what I was hearing.

*Where did that come from?* I didn't understand what was happening, and I started shaking. That ring was my identity. *Why would I ever take off this ring? I'm not moving.* Sometimes, when we're stubborn, we need a little shove to get moving, right? Well, I felt the hand of the Lord on my back shove me off my seat. Again I heard, "Take off your ring and leave it at the altar."

With the shove, I stood up. At this point, I'm on my feet, sobbing. Everyone else was sitting down and listening to the pastor after worship, as I slowly walked up to the front. Pedro was sitting with the worship team, watching me go to the front, wondering what was happening, wondering what was wrong.

When I made it to the front, I looked up at the pastor, shrugged my shoulders, and murmured, "I don't know…I'm just supposed to do this," and I set my ring down on the altar. The pastor asked me, "Does your husband know you're doing this?" I said, "No, because God is telling me to do it."

Scared and devastated, doing this was painful—it hurt. God was asking me to give up something I was holding onto that wasn't serving me. Here I was, waiting for compliments from strangers to fill me up with joy for a brief moment, when everything else inside me felt dead. I was searching for identity and searching for purpose, but that ring was keeping me in bondage.

In His kindness and goodness, God was showing me I had placed this ring on a pedestal, idolizing it, looking to it for a sense of joy, purpose, and identity. It was not cheap; we spent at least $30,000 having it designed and made. Never in a thousand years would I have randomly taken that ring off my finger and left it behind somewhere. *Never.* But looking back, I see how He was expanding me. He was preparing me for who I know I am now, for my identity now, for my purpose now. Against all logic, He was expanding me when He told me to take off that ring.

Soon after I left the ring, it felt like a huge weight lifted off of me, like blinders had blocked me from seeing the truth in front of me. He allowed me to actually love myself—to accept the gifts He'd put in me. Now, instead of seeing myself as *just Mom* or *Pedro's wife*, God told me, "You have a name. You have gifts I've given *you*." For years I dismissed my hospitality gifts as nothing, no biggie, too basic. But I realize now how well my gifts work together with my husband's—he gathers people and I feed them!

In giving up something precious, He was preparing me. With that act of obedience, I believe it broke chains that would have held us back from entering what we were meant to do. From that day on, Pedro and I have continued to lay things down—even things that look good on the outside, but we know they're not right on the inside. Little did I know just how much we needed to lay down or where our lives would go next.

> **That act of obedience broke chains.**

About a year after I left the ring on the church altar, we lost everything—houses, cars, friends, properties, business relationships, millions. We laid everything down until we were bare. Things were dire and unstable, but God had me. I was ready, in some weird way; ready for what we were stepping into. I felt like God saved me when He directed me to leave my ring at the altar. Had He not asked or if I had not obeyed, I would have been forced to sell my precious ring, and that would have done more damage to my fragile self-image. *God, You were so good. You knew this was going to happen. My identity would have still been caught up in that, and our financial crash and burn would have destroyed me and damaged my faith.*

During that year in between, I was able to work on who I was in Him. He knew I would need it. We spent several years in the financial gutter, but thank God I had Jeremiah 29:11 and an identity now rooted in God.

God is patient; He will wait for us to lay things down when He asks. But when we delay, we delay a breakthrough. Do we wait a month? Six months? Years? In our situation, I felt like Pedro held on and delayed the bankruptcy process (which was inevitable). He was deathly afraid of the word *bankruptcy*. Only after all the bankruptcy proceedings were complete was when we saw God shift things. God could finally say, "Okay. Now, let's go." That's when things finally turned around for the better. Delayed obedience because of fear held us back.

Now that He has redeemed our lives and finances, all of the "things" have been restored back to us—cars, homes, material things, and an abundance of relationships and purpose. We are reaping the rewards of lives rooted in Him despite obstacles, pain, and devastation. When He redeems, it's not just getting back what you lost; He brings more. He's so good. When we keep our identity in Him alone, we become trustworthy. Then, He knows stuff won't have us.

For a long while, I thought *I guess I can never wear a ring again* and didn't for ten years. But material things weren't the problem; it was a mindset problem. I was allowing something in my life to stop me from getting where I was supposed to go. God told me, "I never said you can't have nice things. Just don't idolize them; don't allow them to define who you are or stop you from getting where you're supposed to go. Your identity is in Me."

Recently, God brought this ring story back to my memory by saying, "My people have to let things go. They need to leave things on the altar." I doubt He's asking you to leave a ring, so don't worry! But what is it that you've put your trust in or where are you getting your identity from that's not Him? We've all had things holding us back from truly believing we're made for something specific and wonderful. What is it for you?

Maybe you need to lay down a material thing, something financial, a title or position, certain relationships, philosophies of the world, successes, or failures. He'll show you the areas. He wants to shine a light on the false areas where your identity has grown roots.

> **God wants to shine a light on the false areas where your identity has grown roots.**

When I was recently at the ocean, I talked with a woman who was worried about starting a new business. I was able to share about the pure freedom that exists when you step into your identity in God. You're truly free from the "what ifs." *What if I mess up...*" If I mess up, He has my back!

For me, when certain things rise up that might look like the past—maybe a failure or a fear—it's a great reminder of God saying, "Do you remember what I did? Do you remember what we went through together? Do you remember My faithfulness?" Things like doubts and worries can creep up, but all things work out for good. It's so true: ALL things.

About a year ago, we had one of our online challenges not work out well. It bombed! But I'm thankful for our new outlook; our new vantage point. We said, "How can this be turned into something good? What can we do to make it good?" If there's one thing we've learned, it's that God is faithful to work things out. We have the inner confidence of *He's done it for me before, and I know He'll do it for me again.*

You've probably heard people say, "God's got you; you're good." But it really is true. There's hope in knowing this. Once you've seen Him carry you through and work everything out, you wonder why you ever doubted Him. *Why didn't I give You more before, God? Why did I try to carry it all?* He really is our Father. He really does want the best for us and doesn't want us to suffer, be in lack, or live in fear.

**There's a freedom in trusting Him!**

There's a freedom in trusting Him—even if He asks us to lay something down.

## Susan Fujii,
### author, teacher, worship dancer

Born and raised in the United States with a three-year stint in Germany, Susan Fujii now lives in the snow country of Hokkaido, Japan. She has recently published her first book called *Two Sisters: Dementia Caregiving with the Reckless Love of God*, which describes her journey in taking care of her mother and aunt as they battled Lewy Body Dementia and Alzheimer's Disease. This gave her a desire to help those who are alone in caregiving for family members. Whether it's just listening or bringing dinner, she makes herself available to encourage others in their journey.

Susan worked as an accountant in Hawaii until moving to Japan, where she taught English for over 25 years. She serves as a prayer minister, and also as the Praise and Worship Hula (dance) Ministry leader at her church.

Susan enjoys creating choreography as well as sewing clothing and accessories. She loves French roast coffee with a cinnamon roll (or any other sweets), traveling, taking pictures, and pandas. She has also rediscovered her passion for writing and is in the process of writing her second book.

### Connect with Susan today at:

### www.SusanFujiiAuthor.com

# CHAPTER THREE
Susan Fujii

# His Creation Is Perfect

As far back as I can remember, I've been a dreamer. As a child, visions swirled in my head of places to go and things to do. I created my own blueprint of the "dream" home, and when I wasn't satisfied with the layout of a school, I created a blueprint of the "perfect" school. I even designed new clothing for my paper dolls as I envisioned modeling my trendy designs on a fashion show runway.

Reading fiction books also fueled my imagination. Whodunits pulled out the detective in me as I became the world-famous detective searching for the culprit. Joining *Nancy Drew* and *The Hardy Boys*, we traveled the world through dangerous African safari lands, climbed the mountains of the Swiss Alps, and even disguised ourselves in a saree to catch the runaway suspect at the Taj Mahal. I dreamed of writing my own books with daring adventures as I personally visited each country on the planet.

Even school textbooks catapulted me into my own world. Pictures showing the Sahara Desert prompted me to answer, "Go see the transverse dunes in the Sahara!" when the classic question "What do you want to do when you grow up?" was asked. My imagination was my playground, and I visited it as often as time would allow.

Mr. Bennett, my sixth grade teacher while my dad was stationed in Germany, drew out the imagination of all his students with fun projects, and I couldn't wait for his class every day. But one day, a substitute teacher showed up in his place. Mr. Bennett had suffered a compound fracture and would be out for the remainder of the semester. I couldn't understand why, but this substitute teacher was friendly to all the other students except me. She either ignored me or looked at me as though I were unwelcome.

One day, while sitting at my desk, I looked up at my new teacher, and our eyes met. I caught her looking at me, and it was almost as if hatred oozed from her eyeballs. Shaken, I quickly looked away. Questions swirled. *What did I do? Is something wrong with me?*

Longing for an answer, I told my parents when I got home from school. After listening, my dad replied, "You did nothing wrong, and there is nothing wrong with you. She's the one with the problem, not you. Understand?" Nodding, I pretended to understand even though I didn't. *Something IS wrong with me*, I thought, *otherwise she wouldn't just treat me this way.*

From that point, I tried to remain unnoticed as much as possible. I always hid behind the person sitting in front of me in class and never raised my hand or drew attention to myself. If nobody talked to me, they wouldn't know there was something wrong with me. And most of all, if nobody noticed me, I could remain invisible to the world.

My dad got transferred to New Mexico, and starting a new school with new people left me paralyzed. One day, in a high school where I was the only Asian, we studied World War II. It was difficult learning about the bombing of Pearl Harbor in Hawaii and the subsequent atomic bomb on Hiroshima, Japan. It also felt ironic that my dad was from Hawaii and my mom was from Japan. Classmates felt indignant when discussing the unthinkable "kamikaze" bombing on innocent people in Hawaii, and then felt a subsequent righteous satisfaction with the atomic bombing on what they considered a terrible enemy. "They deserved it!" was the consensus.

> **Why did I have to be born like this? Am I really different than everybody else?**

Although unspoken, glances my way made me squirm. Suddenly, a shame, guilt, and dislike for being a Japanese-American filled me from head to toe. *Why did I have to be born like this? Am I really different from everyone else? What is this burden I feel? Just who am I? And that substitute teacher in sixth grade—did she feel the same way as she looked at me in class?* Like the bombs exploding over Pearl Harbor and Hiroshima, everything inside of me seemed to shatter. And on that day, without looking back, I walked away from those shattered pieces and decided to build a different and better "me."

The first step to changing myself was to try out for the high school pom-pom squad. I had envisioned dancing for the Radio City Rockettes as the first 4'-11" bombshell ever to hit the stage. I practiced and practiced. Then, the tryouts came. The result? Only the juniors made the team. All us sophomores would have to wait another year to try out again.

I tried to hide my disappointment, but when I got home my parents asked, "How was it?" I burst into tears and ran into my room. *Why is changing myself so distressful? Why am I always being rejected?* Determined to make something of myself I decided to try out again the following year, but I was met with a resounding, "No!" from my dad.

"Why not?" I demanded to know.

"I don't want to see you cry again," he replied.

"You think I'm going to fail?" I asked, totally aghast by his reply.

"The chances are fifty-fifty. That's too big a risk." I ran into my room, too stunned to even cry. Added to that was the unbearable disappointment when I learned all those trying out for the second time made the team.

Writing was still my passion, so I then threw all my energy into writing for the high school newspaper. I was going to be a famous journalist, as I selected journalism as my major in college. Dreams of covering major events in different countries quickly faded as I cringed each time I received a small assignment that involved interviewing people, and the daring adventures I wanted to write about as I traveled the world seemed to dissipate into thin air.

Not knowing what to do, I settled for accounting. *It's similar to business*, I thought, and I strived to finish college in four years, even though I had to withdraw one semester after the death of my father, who had returned to Hawaii after retirement.

Graduating from college with a bachelor's degree in accounting, moving to Hawaii to help Mom, and then landing a job with what was then a Big Eight Accounting Firm, was the first step in what I thought was the path to my new purpose. On my first day at work, I was handed a big cardboard box containing hundreds of receipts.

"This client hasn't filed her taxes for several years. Sort out her items and identify what her capital gains and losses are for each year. Many personal expenses are in there, so you'll have to discard those," explained my boss, as my jaw dropped in dismay. College textbooks and real life were vastly different, I quickly learned, as I spent days sorting through old receipts.

Tax season was long and grueling. Auditing was tedious and time-consuming. *Soon I'll get my CPA and climb to the top*, I thought as I endured the never-ending hours of number crunching. A co-worker then introduced me to a volunteer organization called the Jaycees. It was a leadership training organization which taught the principles of individual development, management development, and community service. It also intrigued me that their creed began with "We believe that faith in God gives meaning and purpose to human life."

Wanting so much to know the meaning of my life, I jumped at the chance to join. I quickly volunteered at every event I could and found myself leading many events. Being elected as a board member, and finally leading our chapter to the number one position in the state, I kept myself busy, still searching for that elusive meaning and purpose for my life.

> **I wanted so much to know the meaning of my life.**

*Now I can finally change myself.* Keeping myself in leadership positions forced me to be talkative, encouraging, and always positive. Alcohol, especially beer, lifted my spirits, so I went out with "the guys" to the local bars after volunteer events. Shopping for clothes and accessories helped cover the dislike I had for my looks. I purchased a new home and car, as I believed owning these brought meaning.

Then one day, my foundation cracked. I failed the CPA exam. It was more difficult than I had thought it would be, and while taking the exam, I had an uneasy feeling this was not what I really wanted to do. As I talked to an acquaintance about my confusion, she introduced me to horoscopes. "They tell you your future, and it's so accurate!" she exclaimed.

I started to read with excitement each day's horoscope. Some seemed so true that I dug deeper. Then I found there was a correlation between the sun and moon horoscopes based upon the date and time you were born. I dug even deeper. With much anticipation and excitement, I found my reading:

"You will wander aimlessly through life."

*What?!* My eyes widened in shock as I read that over and over again thinking somehow I must have read it wrong. As I started to realize I *had* read it correctly, I hurled the book into the trash can. *This can't be!* Anguish and despair seemed to wrap around my body like a cobra. *Am I really destined to live the rest of my life as a nothing? What value do I have as an aimless wanderer? Why did I have to be born?* These questions played over and over in my mind until I fell asleep in a pool of tears.

The days seemed endless, and even my involvement with the Jaycees came to a screeching halt as I became exhausted trying to maintain the persona of an outgoing person. Except for work, I refused to leave the house. My refuge was in music, which soothed my soul, and Japanese samurai shows where I watched enviously as the ninja seemed to just disappear in an instant.

One day a co-worker came to my desk with excitement in her voice. "You've just got to go here!" she exclaimed, as she handed me what looked like a business card. On it was written "New Hope Christian Fellowship." *A church? Why would I want to go to a church?* I doubted this would help, but her enthusiasm intrigued me. A week later, I found the courage to ask my friend to take me with her to church.

Much to my surprise, my friend took me to the same place—New Hope Christian Fellowship. Instead of wooden pews, there were green plush chairs. Instead of solemn hymn music, there were upbeat songs. I sensed electricity in the air, an anticipation that something good was going to happen. The pastor's message of change penetrated deep into my heart, and as I attended weekly, it felt like refreshing water being pumped into the dry, brittle chambers of this heart which was looking for that elusive change to bring meaning to my life.

> **If felt like refreshing water being pumped into the dry, brittle chambers of my heart.**

The change was abrupt and sudden. My aunt was diagnosed with stomach cancer and relatives weren't sure if she would make it. When asked what her wish was, she replied, "For all of us (Mom, myself, and Aunty) to live together in Japan." Mom jumped at the chance, but I waivered back and forth until I finally felt God was telling me to go.

I had visited several times, but living in Japan was, at first, a nightmare. I looked Japanese, but didn't speak the language. When I didn't understand what was said, the person either shouted or became impatient and rude. Normally fast at retorting, I was left speechless.

Feeling lost and alone, I decided to listen to sermon tapes I had purchased from church before leaving Hawaii. After one of the messages, I decided to change my Bible reading habits. It sounded like a good idea to start the day with the Word—before anything or anyone distracted me. I set my alarm to 7:30 a.m., and the following morning, I was awakened by someone calling my name.

"Susan! Susan!" a deep, but gentle voice called. Startled, I scurried from under the covers and grabbed my Bible. I waited, but heard nothing more so I opened my Bible and started reading. *Was that God calling me?*

Pressure from my aunt to find work forced me to start teaching English. Not looking like a "foreigner," English schools refused to hire me, and I had to learn how to start my own English business. One of my students was the pastor's wife of the New Hope Christian Fellowship Sapporo, Japan, branch. They had a small event at their home church, and my English students and I went to watch.

Rika, one of my students, was very interested in the praise and worship hula we saw at the event, and invited me to join her at a Gospel Hula Workshop in Tokyo. The workshop was scheduled during Golden Week, one of the most expensive holidays in Japan where airline fares and hotel prices drastically increase.

That evening, I started to pray—or rather, complain—to God. "Why does it have to be during Golden Week when everything is so expensive? Why couldn't it be the week after? Or better yet, why couldn't it be in Sapporo?"

Then I heard that same deep but gentle voice, "Do you really want to learn, or not?" *Who's there?* I wanted to ask, but I knew. God was calling me to Tokyo, and there I received the first vision from God in my life. I was in the front of a line of women, all wearing red pa'u skirts, white blouses, and dancing under a bright, bright sun.

Soon after, I was on my first mission trip to Cambodia. Our group wanted to dance the hula and sign language dance I learned at the workshop. I found myself on a second mission trip to India nine months later. This time, we danced in white t-shirts and red pa'u skirts, just like the colors in the vision I had seen. *Is this the meaning of the vision?* I wondered. The following year I was off to Zimbabwe where I danced my first solo in front of three thousand fired up believers at an Easter conference.

It was just before going to Zimbabwe when I learned of inner healing. Listening to tapes and following instructions about forgiving people revealed a shocking memory I had buried deep down inside of me. Dad had been worried about my being an introvert and told Mom, "She's a nice girl, but she has no personality." Everything I learned about forgiving, leaving wounds at the cross, and pleading the blood of Jesus to cleanse me flew out the window. I walked around stunned for weeks.

Then, the voices started. *Ha-ha, no personality. You're a nothing. Who would want you around?* These words played over and over until I desperately cried out to God to just kill me. The deep but gentle voice spoke again, "I gave you a personality. I gave you a quiet and gentle spirit."

At the conference in Zimbabwe, I was slain in the spirit where the Holy Spirit performed massive soul surgery. A stronghold broke over me, and this disdain for myself turned into an appreciation of having "the unfading beauty of a gentle and quiet spirit, which is of great worth in God's sight" (1 Peter 3:4 NIV).

Upon returning to Japan, the hula ministry at our church, ICF, was born. I found my passion. Creating choreography matched my love for music. My ability to sew enhanced my dream to create beautiful hula clothing and gifts. And the wonderful meaning of the vision was revealed: by the blood of Jesus (red skirts) we are made righteous (white blouse), and we are dancing for the glory of God (bright sun).

Although many fun memories were made, there were often many hurdles to cross. I often cried out to the Lord, "I can't do this anymore! Why am I the leader? Why did You choose me?" But I was met with silence.

Then, one day I proposed a 30-day prayer challenge to the members as we tried to discover God in different ways. One of the challenges of the day was "Think of a disappointment that happened in your life. Now, ask God how He feels about it."

I drew a blank. As I struggled to think of one, the time I couldn't try out for the pom-pom squad in high school flashed in my mind. *Hmm, forgot about that.* "Okay, God, how do You feel about that?" I asked, somewhat nonchalantly.

Like in the book of Job when God suddenly spoke out of the storm, I immediately heard, "When your dad saw you cry like that, it pierced his heart. Try to understand his feelings. And that's how the hula team was born. What do you think about that?"

I was floored! Before I even knew God, He had planned to take that bitter disappointment and make it into something amazing. And when I thought about my tears piercing my dad's heart, it seemed as if God was saying He felt the same way when His Son was nailed to the cross. Redemption took on a new meaning.

Daydreaming of the African safari became reality in South Africa and Zimbabwe. Wearing a saree became reality when we were each given one in India, and danced the hula in them. Climbing the Swiss Alps became reality when we took the Jungfrau Railway on a European tour. Walking down a fashion runway became reality when I modeled at a leather shop fashion show in Turkey. And now, this buried passion for writing has risen from the ashes. My imagination playground I had thrown aside was really an invitation to know God.

The more I learned who God was, the more I learned who I was. And the more I learned who I was, the more He lavished surprises upon me. My forgotten dream of visiting the Sahara Desert became a reality as I rode a camel there. I was the last one in the caravan, and as I turned around to look behind me, the transverse dunes I had wanted to go and see "when I grew up" were smiling in magnificent grandeur.

> **The more I learned who God is, the more I learned who I am.**

God sent me to Japan to learn my heritage. Japan is rich in culture, beautiful in nature, and filled with wonderful people. It was also here where I learned my heritage of Hawaii, which also has a rich culture, beautiful nature, and wonderful people. Not only that, but God also sent me to many different countries abounding in amazing cultures with wonderful people. There is absolutely no shame or guilt in being a Japanese-American, and the shattered pieces of myself I had walked away from in high school had now been put back together with the Master's hand, gloriously bonded with His everlasting love.

When we look around, we see flowers and plants of all different colors and call them splendid. We see birds and animals of all different shapes and call them awesome. We see mountains and rivers of all different sizes and call them magnificent. Nature sings of its beauty. And when God looks at all the people He has made in His image, all different ethnicities, languages, and cultures, He sings and calls each one of us His Masterpiece!

## DelShanna Moore,
### author, coach, minister

DelShanna Moore is a movement within herself. Having successfully authored and self-published three books through divine revelation, DelShanna strives to converge and loose those who are held captive by their untold stories. After overcoming many challenges in life, including depression, suicidal thoughts, self-destructive and sabotaging behaviors, enticement with perversion, and alcohol, she is the authority who demonstrates a renewed life.

DelShanna is an Ordained Minister, who exposes God's Word in a way that pierces the stony heart, shatters the walls of alienation, and connects people to the freedom granted by Holy Spirit. She also passionately bears the banners as a signet of God's fresh wind, anointed sound, and presence. Her worship carries power, fire, and deliverance.

DelShanna is the CEO and founding member of Wrapped in His Word created to bring inspirational merchandise by pressing the ear of God and bringing hope and love to the nations. As a licensed coach, mediator, and trainer, she has led many to make decisions and take immediate action in their relationships, marriage, parenting, finances, annual planning, community, and faith-based organizations to reach positive outcomes. Minister DelShanna's gift of faith has been the sustaining force of all transformation and success.

Meet DelShanna on social media, email her at
**delshannamoore@gmail.com**, or visit:

**www.IAamWrappedInHisWord.com**

# CHAPTER FOUR
## DelShanna Moore

# I DO. I DO NOT. I DO!

"Don't say *I do* if you don't!" a group of my friends agreed. I lowered my chin into my chest, looked away, and knew I did not want to marry him. After I left my friend's house that night, I drove to my parents' home with a heavy heart.

On the one hand, *I could marry him and prevent my child from being a "bastard."* My parents were married young and made sure we weren't born out of wedlock. On the other hand, I could accept that I had lost my passion for him and wanted to live a different life. I wanted to explore college and the new world I had entered without him, but my tummy was growing. An unborn baby grew inside me, awaiting the day to be embraced with unconditional love and undivided attention by *both* parents, not just one. *What am I going to do?*

I knew he was marrying me because I was pregnant, and he wanted to honor our families and the church. He wasn't ready for marriage. He enjoyed partying every weekend and spending time with friends. A family? A wife? No, he seemed more excited about living his youth than settling down with a family. Inside, I knew *I do not want to marry him.* My heart was heavy that night as I tried to sleep before the big day.

I thought about calling it off. I tried to figure out how to explain to my parents that I had changed my mind. When I thought of what others would say, I shook my head and knew it was too late. I couldn't bear the embarrassment of calling it off. Feelings of shame and guilt had begun to eat away at my heart. How could I face my family and friends or hear the words of my parents after all they'd done on such short notice to pull off the wedding? And him, the husband-to-be, the mere thought of facing him, looking into his deep brown eyes, caused me pain and tears I couldn't quite explain. I thought about what I would say in front of everyone instead of *I do.* How could I manipulate my wedding day and come out fair?

But I couldn't stand the pain of saying no, disappointing others, or facing my truth. I resolved to follow through with the plan. After all, I didn't want to give back the gifts—*so many have already been delivered to the house.* I was going to get married tomorrow, and I was going to make the best of my marriage and my life.

Tomorrow was my big day. The family was preparing food for the guests and getting the house decorated. Someone altered my dress to fit my protruding tummy holding our little one inside. Six months pregnant, a sophomore at the university, and with a brand-new car, I was about to make one of the most significant decisions in my life. I was going to marry my unfledged high-school sweetheart.

The day began as usual, with sunshine and cool breezes. Family and friends showed up to create their special touch on the house to make everything beautiful for this young bride. Flowers, ribbons, chairs, picture collages of our lifeline, and even more flowers set the day off without a hitch. Everything was perfect. We had food for more than enough people, somebody took pictures of us with all the guests, and the hits flowed with my brother as the DJ. Many enjoyed the backyard dance floor and had a great time. The family and friends in attendance were our most loved ones in the community. My parents' home overflowed with people throughout the house, all through the yard, and gifts flooded the gift table. We spent that night together in a local hotel, and then he had to report back to the Marine Corps while I went back to my childhood bedroom at my parents' home, pregnant and married.

After we married, so many things changed. My stress level increased being responsible for our family. We spent hours on the phone during his military training across the country. Nights were lonely and bearing the pregnancy alone was not quite my dream come true. However, I pressed through and delivered a healthy baby boy. Eventually, his assignment landed in our hometown, and we were able to secure a home for ourselves. Our families were supportive, and we seemed happy and growing as a young married couple.

As years passed, we grew further and further apart. Neither of us said it, but our marriage was a hot mess. We spent more time apart than together. Agreements decreased in the silence of our agitated grunts towards each other. I planned my exit and decided for all of us. Then, I left.

The decision to leave was very calculated and easy. I made the decisions for our family, and this was no different. One of the first things I did was to send our child to be with family and terminated our joint employment venture. In one moment, my future became clear, and it would not include being married to him. My heart had turned callus and my mind was unbendable. I moved out, continued my education, and became a single parent.

> **My heart turned callus, and my mind was unbendable.**

I enjoyed being single. I loved the ability to come and go as I pleased. However, there was a limitation I had as the primary parent: I was a SINGLE parent! *Who in my life can I look to for support and to serve as mentors?* There was no one. Dual-parent households and married couples surrounded me. Even my peers had committed to their spouses and building their families on solid ground. I was hurt. I felt abandoned. I felt ashamed that I was the "only one" in the family who was divorced and a *single* parent.

My first Christmas as a single mom was a challenge. I didn't have much to give or offer that year. During our family gathering I remained distant and sat away from everyone. I tried to smile as others enjoyed themselves and opened many gifts with their children. Trying to hold back the tears and hide the pain from the scars as a divorcee, I felt like a failure, alone, disappointed, and broke. In my best attempts to hide my heart's soreness, my dad saw me.

When my father asked how I was doing that day, I ranted about not being able to compare to the others and only having a few small gifts for my son. As I continued to rant, I released the conviction that I was *the only divorcee in the family*. My father stopped me mid-sentence. "What? Who told you that?" I had assumed married couples in our family were the first and only relationships, but I was wrong. He began listing women and men with multiple affairs, adding names. I was shocked! This correction lifted the burden of shame off of me. I didn't gain a sense of pride for being divorced, but I did gain confidence in knowing I made the best decision possible for my life.

Despite this, I believed God had cursed me to be a single parent. *This must be punishment for my sins and disobedience.* I couldn't fathom how or why a circumstance with such a heavy burden was my lot in life. *God has cursed me with this.* I cried often, fell into depression, wished I was dead, and lived a double life trying to cope with this life as a single parent all while presenting myself as a happy person to others. This season in my life pushed me to seek worldly pleasures and alternatives to my religion. *It's time to find a new me.*

Having been raised in a Baptist church, I enjoyed my Christian upbringing. Church twice on Sundays, choir rehearsal on Thursdays and Saturdays, and an occasional Bible study was the weekly routine. Even when married, I found my way to a few Sunday services, but all that changed as a divorced, single parent. I had a Bible that I didn't understand and a church family who didn't understand me. I refused to trust them enough to share my heartbreak and found myself

> **I had a Bible that I didn't understand and a church family who didn't understand me.**

no longer attending anyone's church meetings. So, I left the church, too.

The club, however, had what I desired. Dancing, alcohol, and being around lots of random strangers was the atmosphere I embraced. I wanted to hide in the crowds yet enjoy the ambiance of soulful music, the dance floor, and a drink or two. With new friends as babysitters, I joined the dating scene and became promiscuous, friendly, and accessible. Seeking love in all the wrong wild places was the best way to describe my time as a single parent during college.

Anger overwhelmed my heart. I was angry with the world and God. Besides, *how could the church or anything aligned with God help me anyway?* I ran from everything I learned from my upbringing. This phase of my life was about finding me, what I liked, and what I wanted—not trying to please others. I survived a traumatic childhood and a failed marriage and became a single parent. Trauma and continual pain led me to very dark places.

I found myself in relationships that didn't match my faith, aligning with people who took advantage of me and used me for their wildest fantasies. I moved in with one guy, had roommates, and enjoyed the nightlife of a 24-hour town. Alcohol became my comforter; drinking daily became my habit, along with entertaining tarot cards, numerology, and other forms of witchcraft to improve my life. Even though I tried to return to church occasionally, it was the "cards" and the "numbers" I followed more than Christ.

During this season, my son went to live with his father. He spent the next two years establishing a relationship with his dad. I spent that time doing everything I felt I couldn't do as a single parent. I worked out daily, changed my eating habits, and lost 30 pounds in less than two months. My heart began to turn toward God as I talked about wanting to attend a church that welcomed me and met new people who loved God.

After finishing my master's degree, a friend invited me to her church. The music, singing, preaching, and people were all welcoming and loving. I hadn't had that much fun in church since I was a child. I felt like I was experiencing something I faintly recalled—an encounter that felt familiar and comfortable. Being in the church that first Sunday felt like home.

*Finally…a place where I feel joy again.* I embraced the lightness of life, and the heavy burdens of my life disappeared when I was at church. I picked up my Bible and began reading it with understanding. I made new friends who also read their Bibles, studied using a concordance, and followed Christ wholeheartedly. The alternative beliefs melted off, and I jumped into the "church" and learned all I could about my Savior, Jesus Christ. Whatever there was to join—the choir, counseling ministry, and ministerial class—I joined it. Practically every time the doors were open I was there, attending every program I knew about, and every church service—up to three times on Sundays. I even jumped in line to be baptized again by the pastor after choir rehearsal one evening to ensure my salvation and to ensure my filthiness was washed away. I got saved "for real" this time. I even obtained the gift of speaking in a heavenly language and learned to seek God in prayer like never before. There was a fire in my eyes; a fire in my belly. My smile was contagious, and I was on fire for God, beginning to walk into realms and dimensions I had never known.

I often went up to the altar for prayer to eliminate every little and big thing holding me back. I was relentlessly pursuing the Kingdom of God, and my church was paving the road for me to meet Jesus. Even so, something remained missing despite all I was doing in the church and at home seeking Heavenly Father. After studying the Word all night and waking early for devotion, I still cried and felt disgusted with my life. Serving at church and being with my new church friends was great, but I could not break the crying, disappointment, and hopelessness deep within me. I was still mean and cold at heart.

**I could not break the crying, disappointment, and hopelessness deep within me.**

Even after my son returned to live with me, there was a distance I could feel from my heart. I could like and love, but only partially; I could celebrate somewhat but never fully. My cynical humor and sly comments would destroy a party scene and challenge those around me. I was hard to love! I was still broken! My heart posture toward God was incongruent to my demonstration of disdain toward those around me. They knew I was hard to love.

Lovelessness was a defensive mechanism built in me from childhood trauma. I did not trust others and could only receive love at the level of my trust in them. My eyes opened as more people challenged my comments and behaviors while proving their unconditional love for me. I recognized they were trustworthy; they sent help, guided, and protected me. They remained loving and consistent, and my heart opened to them. The pain and trauma of my past began to heal, and I was learning how to love again.

Single mom, renting apartments and rooms, living in another state away from my family, working a government job I loved, and married to the church…my life had genuinely transformed, and everyone in my life could see it. Moreover, I could feel it. I knew I was a different person. I called all my exes and repented, for forgiveness. Searching my past, I went through my life and lamented for everything I could think of that I did wrong. I renounced and denounced every witchcraft activity and interaction. I documented my dreams and visions and burned old writings full of demonic impressions. I vowed to celibacy. A new creature, I had surrendered all to God. I was righteous, but more like self-righteous as I journeyed to heal.

For five years I remained celibate, and then I began to question God. I hadn't dated nor accepted any invitations for companionship. Was I to marry again? Was I spoiled goods? Would anyone want me? Was I to remain celibate for another five years? For life? *It's been five years, Jesus. Now what?* No answer. I continued to wait.

A while later, during a celebratory service at a newly joined church, the preacher pointed me out of the audience. The preacher stated that I had been groomed for marriage and was ready to marry. My heart had been so hardened yet longing for a spouse, I turned my face with embarrassment and ignored his prophecy. I didn't believe I was marriage material. *I'm still single for a God-ordained reason, and no one wants me*, or so I thought. About four months later, I met my husband.

The day my aunt-by-marriage came to town, I met her at a church she wanted to visit. Afterward, I drove her and her nephew to her sister's home. The two of us walked to the front door, and I rang the doorbell. A gentleman answered the door, and I extended my hand and said, "Hello," while being introduced as a friend to the family. He didn't let go of my hand as I entered the home. I turned my head to look at him, and, in a vision (supernaturally), I saw his hands waving in circles and him leaning backward. I stopped, looked him in the eyes, and said, "Hello," again. He then released my hand.

The rest of that day seemed similar to a 1950s movie courting scene. I sat with his family, and we shared stories and familial information. We broke bread together and enjoyed each other's company for hours. He asked for my phone number, and I gave it to him. We dated for a few weeks, and then it became apparent there was more happening between us than just friendship.

After seeking the Lord for instruction together, he already knew I was his wife, but I was certain God would explicitly respond to me independently. At home later, I entered my prayer closet and asked God, "Who is he?" I kept hearing a statement repeatedly and continued to ignore it as I prayed more fervently for answers and vision. Then, I heard clearly, "He is your husband..." The Lord responded, and His response settled me. The magnetic force that pulled us together, leaving no space for interference when we met, led us to marry 21 days later as our families blended and our lives transformed.

The disdain that enveloped my heart, the envy I could not remove, and the destroyed stains from my first marriage was erased during my years of walking with Jesus, just the two of us. This allowed my soul the freedom to love. The broken pieces of my personality and thoughts were being molded and mended. My marks of misery and regret were wrong because what I thought was a curse was my blessing. God renewed my mind, allowing me to embrace love, and on our

**Walking with Jesus, just the two of us, allowed my soul the freedom to love.**

September wedding day, 17 years ago, I stood at the altar, looked into his eyes, smiled, and said, "I do!" And I meant it!

God mended my heart; it's no longer broken but healed and whole.

"The Lord is good to those who wait [confidently] for Him, to those who seek Him [on the authority of God's word]."
—Lamentations 3:25

**Cheryl Zalewski**, wife, mother, artist, public speaker

A storyteller at heart, author and artist Cheryl Zalewski seeks to capture the moment, whether through photography, painting, or journaling. From a young age, Cheryl used art as an outlet to express herself after going through a traumatic event, and art became an instrument of healing.

As a young adult, Cheryl loved to travel and visited seven countries before she was 21. When life experiences came along, she found herself married and a mother. This led to unexpected years of homeschooling and single parenting. It also birthed advocacy for domestic violence. Today she continues to create art pieces that inspire hope and healing and has become an advocate for survivors of domestic abuse. She holds art workshops and has been invited to speak at government agencies and continues to be invited to events where she can help bring healing and restoration. Meanwhile, her art expands in mixed media applications, and she's planning a blog to broaden her writing aspirations.

With her new husband, Cheryl enjoys rockhounding along Lake Michigan, photography and being out in nature. She also enjoys indoor activities like thrift and antique shopping, and watching good movies. She currently lives with her husband in Burlington, Wisconsin, and creates handmade art books and journals, paintings and other mixed media pieces that are available on her website.

Learn more now at: **CherylZalewski.com**

# Doormat No More

As I share these events from my life, they read like a movie trailer. My broken chapter, created by layers of the past, eventually reveals a picture.

Despite growing up in a Christian home, though I heard stories about Christ, I rarely, if ever, read them myself from the Bible. Looking back, my beliefs were pretty messed up and I fell into deception. I knew the spirit realm was real; early on, I'd see visions or dream about things happening. One time, when I was about seven, I tried to warn a stranger about something dangerous about to happen. She ignored me, and what I envisioned happened! It freaked me out! Who could I talk to about this? *Who will understand?*

Being involved in seances and playing with Ouija boards as a kid, I became intrigued with a neighbor who knew about the spirit realm. I was drawn into some witchcraft activities out of curiosity and began to take part in and witness things that some only see in scary movies (I won't go into that now). However, letting such things in through my eyes and ears opened the door for further deception and fear. Though still faithfully attending church, I began to trust people and myself rather than my all-knowing, forgiving, loving God, who I didn't even know yet.

Following in my ancestors' footsteps, in my early teens, I couldn't wait to get involved in a secret society that many of them had ritualistically joined. Once again, I got drawn in, received a highly recognized title, and yet so much of it was "secretive."

When I was in ninth grade, events happened in our family, causing us to move from the only home I'd ever known. It was mid semester, during Christmas break. I was devastated by the reasons we'd moved. My mother was dealing with her own pain and separation from her support system. She believed in marriage, and she forgave my father for the reasons we had to start a new life. Back then, I didn't understand. I resented and blamed her for our move.

For me, *Dad couldn't have done anything wrong.* Was that my way of coping? Or did I just not want to know the truth? So many secrets separated us. Inner turmoil was raging. I was in rebellion and confused. *What does love really mean?*

I developed health issues that became debilitating at times, keeping me from participating in activities with family and friends. Loneliness haunted me. My ability to trust people's words and offers of help dwindled, as everyone seemed to have ulterior motives. If I allowed myself to receive help, my mind would be flooded with anxiety, and memories of my once-happy childhood vanished.

> **Everyone seemed to have ulterior motives.**

*What was true?* I was drowning in mind games. I struggled to look good on the outside and got involved in activities in order to be noticed, all while hiding what was going on inside. My inner turmoil desperately needed to find an outlet, and creating art gave me a voice. Granted, not everyone would see or understand my pictures and the pictures within the pictures. At that point, it was okay if the truth remained hidden.

Fast forward to my early 20s. I married a man I cared about, vowing not to be like my father in marriage. I thought I knew it all. Meanwhile, my health issues worsened. Complications of endometriosis made intimacy painful. Doctors prescribed medications to relax me and numb my pain. Yet, the root causes of my problems never got addressed. No one knew. Then, coercion from another, infidelity, more secrets, and fear were factors that conspired to bring about divorce eight years later. The continuing mind- and pain-altering drugs, combined with self-gratifying and unhealthy relationships with men and women, were digging me into a deeper and deeper hole of dysfunction. I now had no idea who I was.

Shortly after my divorce, I chose to marry again. Once again, I trusted a man and his words, ignoring his actions and many warning flags. I didn't really know him, and of course, I really didn't know myself either! My whole definition of love was still questionable. Though something in me knew things weren't right, I'd made a commitment; I was determined to be faithful to it. Warning signs came into sharper focus when I found hidden papers about his past legal issues. I had no idea. I held on. *Surely, things will change.* After I had to have surgery to remove an infected ovary and fallopian tube, he became distant. I thought it was all about me, not realizing the inner turmoil he was facing.

The truth exploded shortly after we learned I was pregnant, and a notification announced him being charged with 4th-degree sexual assault by a former client. I wanted to believe it was an affair gone bad, thinking I could handle that. However, while he was serving time, a second similar charge came through from another woman. Now, I knew I'd have to face this horrifying truth although I didn't want to. Being pregnant, I didn't want to raise this child alone. Because we were still married, I held on. *That's what I'm supposed to do, right?*

For the next six months, I faced morning sickness, lawyers, court hearings, doctors' appointments, bankruptcy proceedings, injuries, and even threats of personal harm from neighbors who were distant, angry, and fearful of the unknown. Newspapers and radio had made my husband's charges public—left me isolated and alone.

But there was something that gave me hope in the midst of the trials. At age 33, I gave birth to a beautiful little girl. It was a glorious day, and nothing mattered beyond that moment. I believe there is grace and forgiveness in the worst of what any of us go through. We've all fallen short, and I still had more falling to do.

Three weeks later, facing hormonal changes, learning to care for my newborn, and dealing with her father's issues, a woman—a friend of mine—came forward with more accusations.

Labels and negative words felt like they defined my existence: Married. Single. Unfaithful. Divorced. Illness. Pain. Legal issues. Bankruptcy. Welfare. Immense fear. Catatonic. Victim. To top that, a police officer called me, telling me that my husband (separated at the time) had been brought in for questioning regarding a previous incident involving injuries to myself and our then 18-month-old daughter. She told me that she'd just put him in jail. With urgency in her voice she stated, "You're in imminent danger! Get a restraining order! Take off your wedding ring and get a new life now!" I was so alone. More court hearings, restraining orders, divorce, disability, PTSD, depression, and medication followed.

Five years later, I joined a religious organization that some would call a cult. It promoted the idea that there were no Christians. I was so deceived. Inner demons manifested. Still trying to hide from reality, isolation from family and friends had become my norm. I was so close not only to spiritual death but also to physical death!

In desperation, I opened myself to deliverance ministers and prayers for forgiveness and salvation. Shackles began to fall off. I was kicked out of the so-called cult (yes, really). Still, I found myself at a crossroads, feeling helpless like I was the walking dead. It took all the strength I could muster to get out of bed each morning.

At the end of my daughter's Kindergarten year, I worked as a school bus driver. One day, I was sitting in the parking lot in an empty bus, with deep thoughts of giving up and ending it all weighing heavily. As I was frozen in my seat like a slow-motion movie, an audible voice with resounding power broke the silence. It declared, "It's no time to be a wimp! It's time to be strong! People are depending on you! Your daughter is depending on you!" Looking in the rearview mirror, I saw no one on the bus but visions of angels filling the seats. I wasn't alone! Things changed that day, with a knowing that God was real. I received more prayer, another chance, and a new beginning. Being assured that I was indeed washed white as snow, I discovered forgiveness was the key! I could finally begin to face myself in the light of reality.

It was a slow process—past situations and events called for me to acknowledge my part in all of it. At first, instead of forgiving myself, I often played the "woe is me" victim role. I had to deal with being a single mom and with supervised visits for my young daughter with her ex-con father. I had a hard time, and I couldn't share all those details with people I met. Shame, resentment, and fear hovered in the background, making me question how God could love me. I was a

> **Shame, resentment, and fear made me question how God could love me.**

sinner, and I knew He hated sin. So, for a long time I thought *He must hate me, too.* I was still dealing with a definition of "love" that sounded and felt more like pain.

Amidst my whirlwind of past lies and deception, God held me tightly, yet oh so gently. He sent others across my path to speak life and truth into me again and again. Wherever I went, strangers shared a word, a smile, or a gesture. People I knew opened up to talk to me about the Lord. Slowly I began to see how blinded I'd been by all my self-concerns instead of care for others. God was undeniably making Himself real to me!

For example, one time I was under a financial burden. At the post office, I received an envelope with no return address. The letter said, "He takes care of His own." There were gift cards for gas, groceries, clothing, and several hundred dollars in cash! The Lord was providing for me beyond measure. A couple also took me under their wing, daily guiding and directing me to God's Word of truth.

Almost unbelievably, the dross of the past began fading away. I was learning who I was, despite where I'd been. I started to have hope for where I was going and learned to trust again—not in people, but in a Heavenly Father. His love was proving to be true in vast, indescribable ways. He was dispelling the lies I'd believed for so long and replacing them with the truth that had always been.

Then, the day came when I started to see myself differently as well as those who had harmed me in the past. It dawned on me that in so many ways, all people have been deceived and believed lies. So, as I was painting the next-door apartment for my landlord, I was praying for the future tenant (which turned out to be me). I was writing positive, blessing words and scriptures on the wall before covering them with paint. Then, I found myself thinking of my ex-husband (not good thoughts I'm sure). Suddenly, God showed me *my* heart. He showed me that I'd been seeing my ex-husband only through the lens of what he had done and not as who he was: a person. God showed me that He could do for my ex-husband what He had done

51

for me and even more!

Previously, I said I forgave him for many things he'd said and done in the past. But, this day, it took root! I truly forgave him. I could say I loved him—not as a husband, but as a person. That day, with a greater power than my own, I loved him with the love of Jesus within me. It didn't mean I had to trust him or ignore set safety measures. But it did mean I no longer held him in bonds to the past. I was allowing God to be in his life, too. I felt so free!

Weeks and months went by. My ex didn't change, and things got worse in phone calls and emails about our daughter. However, I changed! My responses were different. Once, when showing a threatening email to a friend, she asked if he truly had said that. Dishearteningly I answered, "Yes." With her as a witness, I asked God for forgiveness, prayed, and asked for help in responding lovingly to him instead of defensively. My change opened doors to healing and civil communication between us. Again, forgiveness was the key.

Yes, I had work to do. I was still raising a child the best I knew how and learning a new way to live. At last, I was off all medications. Through getting a job as a school-bus driver, I was discovering I had a voice. I no longer had to hide in fear of others' judgments, thoughts, or words. I believe the Holy Spirit made sure I aced both my written and driving tests to secure my job. It allowed me to work *and* take my daughter to and from school. During breaks I would volunteer at the school where she was in special education classes for speech delays, and I got to witness the teacher's tremendous work. I was amazed. They deal with so many different behaviors, personalities, learning styles, and home environments, all with limited curriculum.

My gratitude goes out to the teachers and my God who placed them there. As I was growing in faith, He revealed that several teachers met privately, off school grounds, to pray before classes started each day. They interceded for their students, families, fellow staff members, and what was on their hearts. I know I was someone they prayed for.

In time, I realized—not only through the teachers, but also as a revelation in times when I felt alone, helpless, or misunderstood—I was never alone. God knew. He was there and He sent others—those I knew and those I didn't know—to pray and intercede for a dying soul. Even in times of rebellion, pain, or ignoring my Creator, I had a Papa God lovingly watching over me, patiently waiting for me to receive the love and forgiveness He was so freely giving.

God speaks to me through pictures and His creation. From early childhood, I'd doodle, draw, and paint. Sometimes the subject matter was clear—for example, I love drawing trees. Mostly, however, my works were abstract. It was a way to pass the time, to let go, escape reality, or just be in the moment. Later, while raising my daughter, it was a safe way to process emotions. Then, a time came when those pictures revealed a part of me that had been hidden deep within my being. Repressed memories I wasn't aware of emerged as disturbing images. I remember a day of great frustration. Rage welled up within me, and I started throwing paper on the floor and covering it with red paint. I stomped and stomped on it until my strength was depleted. It felt like I was throwing all the negative emotions under my feet. All the hurtful labels I or others had put on me were on that paper. With this red, angry mess, I was declaring, "Doormat no more!"

**Rage welled up within me.**

Now, for nearly two decades, that work of art has been on display at a local resource center. So much healing and growth has taken place since then. Nevertheless, I found those negative words and labels from the past still had a hold and showed up in my conversations. The Lord started showing me the power of my spoken words, especially when I responded to being asked, "How are you?" I've now learned to proclaim wellness and positive words. It's a conscious choice.

Now, I avoid labels. They leave people stuck in a mindset of the past, frozen in time with a belief system that doesn't change, hoping for something different but never attaining. *Been there, done that.* I've been on both sides of the spectrum—from thoughts of "ending it all" to knowing a loved one who did: my daughter's father.

He was a person, a hurting man, someone who "felt" the painful, deadly effects of labels. He was never able to break free. Yet, I've been guilty of both proclaiming and receiving such labels. On purpose or not, once spoken, the damage is out there in an abyss of intertwining events that can't be taken back. Labels can become a vicious cycle. A choice to end the labels must be made—not to end a life, but to put an end to the feelings of hopelessness that labels reinforce.

Five years ago, I reconnected with a man I knew in high school. We started to date. This time, God was revealing that I could trust again in a man's love. I could give and receive. God was showing His love for me through another human being.

During our courtship, a local women's shelter where I had been volunteering asked if I'd like to create a work of art for Domestic Violence Awareness Month. This time, I placed my canvas outside on the ground and kneeled beside it. With paint, dirt, leaves, shoes, hands, and feet, I intentionally no longer poured out rage onto that canvas as the previous time, but rather love and acceptance. Layer upon layer, it was a meditative time of beginning to fully understand that no matter what I'd been through, my loving Heavenly Father God was always there.

New "Doormat No More" artwork emerged, giving a glimpse of hope, letting go, and stepping out of the cycle of lies that kept me in bonds. It became a piece of transformation and hope. The man I was courting (now my husband) saw the finished painting and said, "I've not walked in your shoes, but I've been in the shoe store." I was not alone! That statement prompted another dimension to the painting.

Negative words and labels were written on the insoles of more than 50 pairs of donated shoes, now piled on the floor below the painting.

Those shoes represent things each of us, regardless of age or gender, experience. We've all "been through things" we'd rather wipe away, leave behind, forget, and go on from. Though scars may remain, memories of the past need not keep us bound. We can leave them at the door, at the foot of the cross, and walk boldly into our new beginning. However, if we carry hurtful things inside, they can't be dressed up by fancy shoes or outward appearances. We each must choose our path for transformation, truth, forgiveness, and redemption. As we step out boldly, we realize the full picture: there's hope in God's love and life.

> **Though scars may remain, memories of the past don't need to keep us bound.**

**Debi Shannon**,
businesswoman,
prophetic consultant

Author Debi Shannon lives in the Dallas/Fort Woth area and has four grown children and five grandchildren. For many years, Debi worked in corporate healthcare, but currently she enjoys helping people through her entrepreneurial strengths. Debi currently manages Shannon Insurance as well as owning Redeemed Solutions. Redeemed Solutions' mission is to serve businesses and individuals by providing resources to maximize personal and professional success.

Redeemed Solutions provides multiple resources to increase profit margins for business owners; assists with gold and silver investments and facilitates alternative real estate options, and more.

Additionally, Debi is passionate about seeing people ministered to and impacted through her prophetic consulting platform, Redeemed Solutions Consulting. This service helps people receive breakthrough in their personal and professional lives.

Visit Debi's website at:

**www.RedeemedSolutions.com**

# CHAPTER SIX
Debi Shannon

# Sow in Tears, Reap in Joy

That summer was a very unique time in my life. We would get together with a very special friend or two every Saturday to worship, write songs, and worship some more. Occasionally, we would add a week night in there as well. Saturday morning, we would start with brunch around 10 a.m. Sometimes we would have dinner and go back to worship. Sometimes we would just have dessert; but we never left before 10 p.m.—more often it was closer to midnight. Usually, the evening would end with me barely able to move to get to the car, still laughing and talking about how the clock *must* be broken! There was no way we just spent 11-12 hours worshiping Jesus. It was a very precious season. Even though I could feel the divine appointment tug, I had no idea what the Lord was really doing. He was pouring into me for what was about to happen.

Life seemed to be pretty normal. Then that fall, everything changed—normal vanished. What we would have given to have normal again! My youngest son, at the age of 28, got the call while at work that the small spot on the bottom of his foot was cancer—melanoma. We quickly found out that if you are diagnosed with melanoma on the palm of your hand or bottom of your foot—where the sun doesn't usually get you—it is very serious.

This story is not from his perspective. I am sure he would have different aspects that he'd highlight or areas he might feel were more pertinent for sure. If he wrote it, it would definitely be longer than a chapter. But this is a story that needs to be told.

As parents, often our children's battles become ours, and this diagnosis was a battle for me to overcome, too. We overcome by the blood of the Lamb and the word of our testimony.

After the initial testing, we learned he had mutation-wild type melanoma. In plain English, that meant they really didn't know how

57

to treat him. There were no drugs for this particular kind of cancer. So few people get this kind of cancer, it doesn't rank as a priority for drug trials.

*I was numb. How can this be happening? How can my son, my baby boy, have cancer?* In the past, I had cancer, and it was not a picnic by any means. But that was different; that was *me*. Truth be told, I will pray for anyone in a heartbeat, but I cannot deal with seeing people in pain, especially if I love them. The thought (and reality) of seeing my child suffer was a crushing weight to me. I was constantly asking God, "Why is this happening? Why are You allowing this? What are YOU doing in this?"

I was thanking Him ahead of time to bring us through, declaring His victory in this situation. I could not allow myself to think anything other than victory. It was GO-FIGHT-WIN mode for me. There was no off switch.

> **God, why are You allowing this?**

We had no idea what we were in for. Life became an endless series of doctor appointments—most of whom did not know what to do—labs, PET scans, surgeries, life-threatening interventions, and prayer. Shortly after the diagnosis, he had his first surgery to remove the tumor on his foot. This wasn't very successful because there wasn't enough skin on his foot to ensure safe margins. Further testing was done to see how far the cancer had spread. The cancer had made it to his lymph system, indicating he was at stage 3C, and it was spreading up his leg to his groin. This meant amputation was not an option.

A week or so later, he met with the plastic surgeon about a skin graft for his foot. He got home from this appointment, walked in the door, and about two minutes later I realized something was wrong. My son looked like he was going into shock. I knew we needed to act quickly. Once at the ER, the doctor told me he didn't know what to do with him. My son received three doses of pain medication in the ER, however still did not get any relief. No mother wants to accept that she has to sit and watch her child suffer.

Growing up, I didn't have much family around. So, when I started having a family of my own, well, they were my world. In fact, I probably overdosed on the Mom gene. There are quite a few people besides my own children who call me Mom. It is a privilege to be in people's lives like that. We almost always had extra kids at our house and never knew how much pizza we would be buying on any given weekend. There were also many times when people lived with us for a season. For the longest time I thought my ministry was laundry and dishes! I have always felt things very deeply (maybe intensely is a better word). I am sure, in many respects, my children feel like that part of my personality is a pain in the (their) butt. But in this moment at the ER, the Mom gene kicked in.

I told the doctor, "I know what kind of shape my son was in when we brought him in, and I'm not taking him home that way, so you'd better find out what is wrong, and do something about it." As the ER doctor and the surgeon discussed the situation, I overheard the conversation: "Admit him for observation to appease the mom." Turns out my son had an infection caused by a staph bacteria, (MRSA). Thirty-six hours later, he was having emergency surgery to remove the extremely large, infected tissue. Intervention number one. God was faithful!

He was in the hospital for Thanksgiving, which was extremely hard for all of us. Everyone in the family came to see him, but his feeling was just that it was all very sad. We were all hurting for him and admittedly didn't handle it very well. I remember Christmas that year. I was so humbled—and quite frankly heart-broken—when I found out he had taken a friend with him to go Christmas shopping and *walked* through five stores in search of the *perfect* Christmas gift for me.

His pain management was nowhere close to being under control. At this point, he had a wound vac to help his leg heal from the surgery. Home Health would come to change it regularly, and he would take everything he could for pain before they came. As they changed it, he would scream and cry in agony. I would be at the other end of the house in my bathroom, covering my ears and crying out to God for grace and help. He celebrated New Year's Eve that year by getting the wound vac off. Not exactly the way his friends were celebrating, I am sure, but he was happy about it. Not many of his friends came around in those days. I know life gets busy, or maybe they just didn't know how to relate to him or what to do. That was one of the unexpected side-effects of having cancer that hurt him as much as the physical pain, I believe. It was a very lonely time for him.

Later, I had a revelation. No one wants to be in a desperate situation like this, right? But I realized that to really experience a miracle, you have to first be in a place where you *need* a miracle to allow you the opportunity to see that facet of Jesus revealed. When we have a need, He can meet it. Experiential knowledge is priceless! It will change your life forever.

> **When we have a need, Jesus can meet it.**

There were dozens of people praying for my son during this time. Family, friends, our church family, entire congregations—some were strangers to me, but they were friends of friends. And yet for me, the only thing I could focus on was talking to Jesus. He was the *only* one I knew who had the power to change this situation.

The following spring, he had another surgery to remove lymph nodes and do the skin graft. Then, in early summer they started him on a drug trial. This process was daunting; it consisted of a lot of red tape, paperwork, and literally signing his life away. The first time dealing with this, it hit my heart hard. After one treatment, the symptoms were life threatening, and he was removed from the trial. The tumors continued to grow.

He had another surgery to take off a massive tumor on his ankle; this was done solely for comfort's sake. By this time the tumors had started to grow higher up his leg. My son asked the surgeon if he could do anything about those. It was clear the surgeon was shocked by what he saw, and quickly replied that there was nothing he could do. Late fall, my son was entered into another drug trial, but that did not produce positive results either, so he was removed from that trial as well. We were all feeling the weight of how serious this was continuously growing to be.

In hindsight, now I realize I was only adding to his pain. I was constantly looking for natural things to help, asking him to try one naturopath thing after another. One day he said to me, "Mom, you've made our whole relationship about cancer." Oh my gosh, he was right! I had been on the offensive so much, focusing on the battle, wanting to do anything I could do to help, that I'd been neglecting the present moments I had with him. I needed to engage with the son who I loved. So, I had to back up and re-group.

Deep down in my heart, I knew there was another issue I was dealing—or more accurately, *not* dealing with. Did I really trust God in this impossible situation? Thirty-two years prior to this, I had a child go to Heaven unexpectedly. I was 37 weeks pregnant; it was Christmas Eve, and she was stillborn. I had buried one child. I know there are so many people who have experienced devastating or similar circumstances. It is undeniably a group you don't want to be a part of. God had brought me through that painful experience. But what I wrestled with now was *I buried my child but never got to know her.* Although there was much sadness and other things to deal with, there was no personality or memories together to miss. The thought of potentially losing my son after 28 years of invested relationship was inconceivable. That was *not* an option. Did I trust God, really?

That December, he somehow got a Strep B flesh-eating virus. This sounds like a Sci-Fi story now, doesn't it? At this point, his medical team thought he had close to 100 tumors. They likened it to leprosy. Wound control did not know what to do with him. During this time, the palliative care doctor took this opportunity to really try to get on top of the pain management, thankfully.

Christmas came, and he was in the hospital. That was one of the worst Christmases of my life. My other children were supportive. They made a digital cut-out picture of my son getting IV's, with a thumbs-up pose. They took that cut-out and inserted it into multiple family photos on Christmas Eve. It was really creative! His siblings flooded him with text messages of what they had done. They wanted him to know he was still part of us, even though he wasn't there physically.

We went to the hospital Christmas morning with his wife. Not too much was said on the long, surreal drive. It just didn't seem possible; how could all this be happening? We got to the hospital and learned that the doctor's game plan was to give him doses of continuous pain meds while being monitored. Then, they'd gradually bring the dosage up every one or two days until they found the combination to successfully manage his pain yet allow him to be functional. It was very hard to see him that medicated.

I don't know how much of Christmas Day he remembers, but I remember. There were doctors who would come in just to see the *abnormal patient* on the sixth floor. They'd look at him, shake their heads, and walk out. Because of his rare condition, he had a reputation—and *not* the kind you want. His wound care became his personal project because no one knew how to best take care of him. His wife tried to put on a smile. We had taken Christmas presents to him. We also brought his ukulele (my family is very musical). The highlight was when a harpist came in his room and played, and then he joined in with her on his ukulele. Somehow, he made it through this. Intervention number two. God is faithful!

Early the next year he was on IV antibiotics, and he started losing weight. He was unable to keep any food down. It was a long season of him eating and then paying for it, constantly. He was in the hospital again, this time primarily for his stomach. He had dropped 40 pounds from his 5'-11" frame. This was so hard to watch, and there was no explanation as to why he was unable to keep food down. Around this same time, he started a third treatment. He had one or two doses, and it seemed to help. The tumors were starting to shrink from baseball size to quarter size.

A couple of weeks later, he wasn't feeling well and somehow managed to drive himself to his oncologist's office. That was a divine appointment. The oncologist was looking at his labs and asked what they had done in the hospital for his liver. He replied, "The doctors never said anything about my liver." The oncologist's countenance totally changed. My son was in liver failure, and the doctor said they needed to do something *right now*! They stopped the drug treatment because, although the drug was helping the tumors, it was killing his liver. His oncologist made it clear that if he hadn't come into the office that day, we would have been having a funeral in 48 hours. Intervention number three. God is faithful!

I had lived the last three years with him constantly on my mind.

> **How can I possibly enjoy anything while he suffers?**

If I found myself enjoying something, I immediately felt guilty. *How can I possibly enjoy anything while he suffers?* There were almost nightly prayer walks where I could openly pour out my frustration to the Lord without it impacting my son. Those walks were sometimes long—with a lot of words on my side of the conversation—but I would come back home filled back up, reassured that God was smack dab in our midst. I was expecting Him to show Himself strong on my son's behalf.

The next summer, they attempted a fourth drug treatment. This protocol consisted of more than 30 injections directly into the tumors during each treatment. He said it was something like a horror movie. There were no results from this treatment.

In the fall of the third year after the diagnosis, his doctors started a fifth treatment—this was his last one. The plan was to be on this treatment for three months. We seemed to have hit a plateau. Then, we got the news. It was at this point they told him there wasn't anything else they could do for him. We were out of options. The treatment was lengthened to six months, and then it was pushed to nine. He had been on the drug three times longer than recommended. His oncologist told him he honestly didn't know, with this being a newly released drug, if it was safe to take him off of it or not. At this point, the next PET scan was scheduled.

This was an all-time low. Everything that he had suffered and had been through had culminated to this point. Five surgeries, two drug trials, three newly released FDA treatments, every PET scan, every single prayer, every declaration, every hope, every fear, every tear, every victory, every set back, had brought us to this point. I say "us" because our entire family was impacted by his journey. Where you go, your family goes with you. We are not put on this earth to be isolated. You cannot fulfill your destiny alone. Whether it be a natural family or a supernatural, God-given family, we need each other!

I remember it was a Wednesday, two days before my birthday, when he went for the PET scan. I spent that day in prayer; *nothing* else mattered. The next day, the report came back. I held my breath while he told us that the PET scan came back CLEAR! Tears flowed and flowed—more as each person in our family heard the news. This outcome was totally unexpected, not only by him and his wife, but by all of his medical team as well. This was a true miracle!

The next day was my birthday. Jesus gave me the absolute *only* thing I wanted as a gift! He is so faithful! I tell my son he is my birthday present every year now. At the time of this writing, he is almost six years cancer free. There were more biopsies afterward to confirm the scan. He lost close to 90 pounds before we later found out the inability to keep food down was due to the drugs, resulting in Celiac disease.

The doctors initially told him to be prepared to be on opioids for the rest of his life due to the extremely high dosage he was on. He almost endangered his life afterward trying to come off the drugs too quickly. It took him almost two and a half years to get off the pain meds. But God is faithful! I am thankful for the medical professionals who were so instrumental in saving my son's life. One of his doctors kept the pictures documenting my son's journey to use in teaching. They are graphic. In hindsight, my son noted God's timing. Had he been diagnosed six months earlier, the last newly released FDA drug would not have been available and he may not be here today.

If you are reading this, if you are breathing, God has a purpose for your life! He has a purpose for you to be on this earth at this time. Sometimes we go through things we don't understand. Sometimes it is painful—very painful. Psalm 46:1 says, "God is our refuge and our strength, a very present and well-proven help in trouble." I know this is a true statement.

At one point, they told my son he only had about a year to live, but that was not how I was praying. Hebrews 11:1 (AMP) says, "Now faith is the assurance (title deed, confirmation) of things hoped for (divinely guaranteed), and the evidence of things not seen [the conviction of their reality—faith comprehends as fact what cannot be experienced by the physical senses]." I'm certainly not an expert on faith, but I do know it's easier to go through life with it than without it. Again, He is faithful!

> **God has a purpose for you to be on this earth at this time!**

The following is my son's post to those who were committed to pray for and encourage him. It is the word of his testimony:

*"The moment we've all been waiting for...Thank Jesus! My cancer is finally in remission! The news was very unexpected—by myself and my physicians. Celebrating and shedding tears with the family was, and well, there are no words. But since my case has been rather strange, even from the start, it took quite a while to verify my initial report. It took more scans and biopsies/surgeries and waiting for the chemo to clear out of my system, which sometimes would take up to three-four months, etc. I'm still a bit weak and coming off certain drugs has been difficult. Also, I know there's a lot for me to reflect on from my journey the last three years. And I would love to share some of those things with you all as I work them out. But all in all, I'm loving life, excited for the future, and just trying to enjoy every moment possible. I'm just happy to be alive and loved by so many people. Thank You All."*

**Mark Pollish**, ski professional, author, coach, prayer warrior

Recently retired, Mark Pollish worked for over 50 years in the ski industry at the Snowbird and Alta ski areas in Utah. For the last 40 years, Mark was a professional ski patroller during ski season at Alta and worked in management year-round for the last 30 years. In 2004, Mark co-wrote Alta's first Environmental Report. He has witnessed many avalanches, rescues, and life-altering situations in the Wasatch Mountains of Utah.

Along with his passion for environmental stewardship, Mark is an avid proponent of personal development. His keen insight into life's purpose or vocation came from a lifelong search through mysticism, travel, adventure, drugs, and music while growing up during the hippie movement of the 60s and 70s. Mark's memoir, *Living the Dream*, chronicles his life story with candor, triumphs, tragedies, and humor (available on Amazon in the summer of 2023). Through his book and ministry activities, he has a passion for encouraging others find and live their dream.

Mark, his wife Carol, and their two dogs live near the mouth of Little Cottonwood Canyon in Utah. Mark and Carol raised their son and daughter to be skiers and now have a grandson who they are teaching how to ski. Since retirement, he now focuses his time on life coaching and personal development.

Contact Mark through his website at:

**www.MarkPollish.com**

CHAPTER SEVEN
Mark Pollish

# The Songs of Change

Packed in between my brother and sister in the backseat of my parents' 1963 Chevrolet Bel Air, suddenly a smooth and gentle melody filled my consciousness. The invitation was compelling for my wild, 13-year-old spirit: "If you're going to San Francisco, be sure to wear flowers in your hair." I closed my eyes as the AM radio station continued to draw me in; people were in motion and summertime in San Francisco was promised to be a love-in. *If only this lengthy car ride could miraculously deliver me at the intersection of Haight and Ashbury in San Francisco instead of our destination—Salt Lake City.*

1967 was the Summer of Love, and my family was moving for the fifth time since I was born. Each place we'd lived in my short 13 years—Montana, Chile, Arizona, Missouri, and British Colombia—had all been accompanied by music. I was raised with a love of music. But in 1967, things were changing, and the music was driving the change. The raw and escalating soundtracks promised freedom and rebellion. Each new song exploded into my imagination and created my dreams.

I sank further into the backseat and into the visions of the Summer of Love blossoming in sunny California. I could barely hear the swishing of the windshield wipers and the pounding of the rain slapping the roof of the car. As we sloshed across the border from Canada into the U.S. near Bellingham, Washington, that day in June, I dreamed of joining the hippies in California. I could see the sunny beaches where I'd surf every day, accompanied by girls in bikinis, amazing, new music, and without bossy parents. *What would it be like to live a carefree life of peace and love?*

As the song ended, the DJ announced the upcoming three-day rock concert—the Monterey Pop Festival—being held just south of San Francisco.

"Hey, Mom, can I look at the road map?" I asked.

"Here you go, Mark," she said, passing it over the seat to me. "See how far it is to Salt Lake City."

Instead, I scanned the map for the best route to Monterey as the DJ listed the names of the performers. The Byrds, my favorite band, was going to be there. My brain ticked off the groups I recognized: The Mamas and the Papas, The Who, Simon and Garfunkel, and Jefferson Airplane. But The Grateful Dead stopped me cold; I hadn't heard them on the radio yet—though many years later, I saw them in concert and came to appreciate their alternative style of music. But for now, I wondered about the strict lifestyle I was being plunged into. Salt Lake City was referred to as "Behind the Zion Curtain"— definitely slow and repressive. A lifetime away from California fun and sun, featuring rock festivals with my favorite bands and blasting out my favorite songs.

I was brought back from my state of California dreaming with the scream from the "Wild Thing" song. The heavy guitar riff grabbed my attention. I sat up and leaned forward. My Dad reached up to turn the dial to another station.

"Dad," I protested, "I really like that song. It's the Troggs."

He turned the volume down a couple of notches and asked, "What did you call them? The Frogs?"

I laughed. All the new bands coming out since The Beatles had weird-sounding names: The Byrds, The Monkeys, The Yardbirds, The Rolling Stones, The Doors. It could be anything: The Supremes, Smokey Robinson and the Miracles, Eric Burdon and the Animals, The Who. My Dad muttered something about this *not being music* but left it on for my sake.

Music was a huge part of my childhood. My parents always had the latest vinyl albums, but this new sound was totally different from the early rock 'n' roll music of Elvis, Chubby Checker, and other artists from the late '50s and early '60s. This new rock had a cutting edge that took me into another dimension. I didn't know where this music-fueled journey would land me, but I knew there was no slowing it down. Like a train picking up speed, I was headed down the track in a direction that would unfold before me in unforeseen ways.

The 1960s were a time of immense change in my generation and in U.S. culture. The controversial Vietnam War instigated heated arguments between fathers and sons. The Cold War was also heating up. There were monumental changes in technology, especially in the space race between the U.S. and the Soviet Union.

The music scene changed, too, as singers and songwriters became more vocal in their political and cultural views. This outspoken discontent, combined with explosive and unusual sounds, fueled my growing desire to see changes in the status quo. The Who released a song called, "My Generation" that summed up the passionate feeling of my youth. I watched on television as peaceful civil rights marches turned into violent race riots in major cities. Amid the quagmire of my parents' generation, I sat desperately watching the turmoil of this rapidly unraveling world. I felt hopeless and without a voice. *Is there hope anywhere?*

I fondly remember John F. Kennedy saying we would put a man on the Moon by the end of the decade. I also remember the day we found out he wouldn't live long enough to see it happen. During grade school, our principal came over the intercom to announce the news. We sat in stunned silence for a minute that seemed like an eternity. President Kennedy's death was the spark that started me questioning the cultural establishment of that time. My parents and I followed the chaos on the nightly news with Walter Cronkite as the Vietnam War escalated and violent protests exploded on college campuses. The infamous Summer of Love was anything but lovely. The following year it got worse. The assassinations of civil rights leader Martin Luther King Jr. and presidential candidate Bobby Kennedy shattered any optimism. Next, the outbreak of a worldwide flu pandemic from Hong Kong killed millions and added to my anxiety.

**We sat in stunned silence for a minute that seemed like an eternity.**

Our embattled nation was hungry for some good news, which finally came on Christmas Eve, 1968. The United States launched its first manned mission to reach the Moon. Roughly a billion people tuned in to watch astronauts Bill Anders, Jim Lowell, and Frank Borman broadcast live from the Moon's orbit, revealing stunning views of the Earth rising over the Moon's horizon. I vividly remember the crew reading from the Bible as they were in lunar orbit. They read verses one through ten from the Genesis account of creation. When they finished reading, Borman added, "And from the crew of Apollo 8, we close with good night, good luck, a Merry Christmas, and God bless all of you—all of you on the good Earth." It would be one year later when Apollo 11 successfully landed men on the surface of the Moon, fulfilling President Kennedy's challenge.

Many people said the successful Apollo 8 mission saved the year 1968—a year full of race riots, pandemics, families fighting over competing ideologies, wars, and rumors of war. Sound familiar? Solomon, the wisest man to ever live, said there is nothing new under the sun. The world's current chaos may prove Solomon's wisdom to be true. Is history repeating itself?

My generation tried to change human history. Us Baby Boomers came from the increase in population after the second World War. Both of my parents served during WWII: Dad in the United States Army and Mom in the American Red Cross. Theirs' is known as the Greatest Generation. They grew up during the Great Depression and became young adults during the War. They were characterized by a strong work ethic and respect for authority. My generation produced the bumper sticker that said, "Question Authority." We challenged the status quo during the tumultuous 1960s. I remember arguing with my dad over social issues like the Vietnam War, antiwar protests, and the civil rights movement.

My generation was hoping to change the world with peace and love. At the time, I was convinced of my way of thinking. I believed there *was* something new under the sun. *My parents are just old-fashioned and stubborn.* Little did I know that time would prove them correct, and I eventually

> **My generation produced a bumper sticker that said "Question Authority."**

abandoned my self-serving way of life. But for the next couple decades, this train I was riding was out of control and not bound for glory. When my family moved to Salt Lake City in 1967, I was already involved in drinking, smoking, cussing, stealing, and causing mischief. Trouble had no problem finding me. I was already walking on the wrong side of the tracks.

One redeeming quality of Utah, fortunately, was the incredible snow and powder skiing. For the next 50-plus years, this sport was my salvation. During my high school years, my friends and I hit the major ski areas every chance we had.

After graduation, I enrolled in the University of Utah and continued skiing. That year, the Snowbird **I became a partier and a drug addict.** Ski Resort opened for the 1971-72 ski season with a world class 3,000-foot vertical rise tram. *This will be the highest high I can imagine.* I thought skiing was good during my high school years, but the following seasons blew my mind in more ways than one. During my years at the U, my friends and I got part-time jobs at Snowbird for the free ski passes. This turned my four-year degree into a seven-year endeavor. I also became a partier and a drug addict. This took me to the deepest, darkest lows in my desperate search for significance in a world rocked by wars, protest, violence, and instability. I did not recognize the power of drugs and a wild partying lifestyle. I was young, confident, and full of certainty that *I'm in control and can stop at any time.* Neil Young's number-one hit song about salvation became my anthem at the time. I, too, was searching for my "Heart of Gold."

My heavy drinking started my senior year of high school. The summer after, a friend introduced me to hash and marijuana. We experimented increasingly with drugs and alcohol and became stoners during college. Whenever we finished a joint, someone inevitably asked, "Where are we going?" "To hell if we don't change our ways," my best friend quipped every time. Ouch, that always stung me.

I lived at home during my freshman year of college to save money. One Saturday night, I obtained some LSD to take before going to a big party. Lysergic acid diethylamide, also known as acid, is a hallucinogenic drug that alters thoughts, feelings, and awareness. Wanting to get an early start on my high before the party, I dropped the acid just before dinner. Bad idea. My sister teased me as I started to trip.

"Hey, Mark, the walls are moving," she taunted. "They look like snakes."

"Be quiet," I hissed, "Mom and Dad will hear you."

Paranoid, I left my unfinished dinner plate and went outside to wait for my friends to pick me up. Mom intercepted me, told me to be careful, and said goodbye. That evening turned into a nightmare. On the way to the party, my friends lit up a joint and laughed as I told them about dinner. There were even more libations at the party—kegs of beer and hard liquor flowed freely. Three Dog Night's song "Mama Told Me Not to Come" rang in my head and soon became my reality. Although most of the party goers were having a good time, my anxiety grew because of the LSD. I nervously talked to a young lady as the music got louder and felt increasingly claustrophobic. Black Sabbath's "Paranoid" blared so loud we could not hear each other.

She sensed my growing paranoia and invited me outside to get some fresh air. In my drug-altered state of mind, I wrongly thought she was hitting on me. Her voice sounded like an echo chamber. The next thing I remember is running after her into the party. Not realizing she'd slammed the glass door shut behind her, I crashed through the glass, buck naked, though I somehow avoided injury, with shattered glass all around me. *When did I take my clothes off?* My friends pinned me to the floor and wrapped me in a blanket, trying to calm me.

I was having none of it. Screaming, kicking, and fighting with superhuman strength, I would not stop yelling obscenities, cursing them, and cursing God. It was like I was possessed by some vile, evil spirit that would not shut up. My friends stuffed several reds—Secobarbital, an obsolete sedative—into my mouth, until finally I passed out. Sunday morning, I woke up on the floor at a friend's house with a nasty hangover. There was no way to hold my head that didn't hurt. Johnny Cash's "Sunday Morning Coming Down" took on a whole new meaning and a revelatory perspective on my life.

Following my dad's footsteps, I had chosen geology for my college major. But school took a back seat as I followed my passion for skiing, rock concerts, partying, and traveling. Still, I had the burning question: *What is the purpose of life? Studying to get a degree and then working hard to be successful? Partying, skiing, traveling, and trying to have fun? Becoming prosperous and using your resources and talent for a worthy cause? Aren't all of these just vanity without one's true purpose?*

During the summer of 1976 a friend and I backpacked through Mexico all the way to South America for five months. Returning to Utah, I switched my major to geography and earned my degree two years later. My parents were relieved and happy their wayward son finally finished college. So was I. But what was next? Broke, with no car and no place to live, I hitch-hiked up to Alta to ponder my future. At the Alta Lodge, I saw a ski touring buddy of mine who was a chef there. After telling him my dilemma, he told me I could work there for the ski season with meals, a room, and a ski pass provided.

For the next two years I worked at Alta in the winter and traveled through South America in the summer. After that, I was a dispatcher with the town of Alta. Then, I became an EMT and joined the Alta Ski Patrol. This was the best ski job one could hope for, but I still wanted to learn. Looking back now over my 45 years working at Alta, it gave me that chance. I learned more about skiing, avalanches, and environmental science than I ever did in the classroom.

After college, I believed life was about having fun. My friends and I worked hard, partied hard, skied all winter, and traveled during the summer. However, I had to ease off on my partying lifestyle after joining Alta Ski Patrol. The job was demanding, strenuous, and required focus, especially when working with explosives and avalanche mitigation. Still, I was not satisfied. Skiing unlimited powder, setting off big avalanches, and taking summers off to travel was not enough. But my life changed for the better in 1985.

Returning to Salt Lake after a summer of traveling, I visited a friend's house to get high. While there, I noticed his wife sitting on the stairs reading a Bible. *Strange.* She was a wild radical like the rest of us, and I'd never seen her read the Bible. Mentioning that I occasionally read the Bible myself, she asked. "Oh really, you want to come to church with me?"

"Sure, why not," I said, thinking it would be like the times I occasionally attended church as a kid. The following Sunday we walked into an old brick building on the west side of downtown Salt Lake City and found our seats. A couple of long-haired hippies my age picked up guitars and violins, and another musician sat down at an old piano. I felt right at home as they began. This group of hippies had moved to Salt Lake from California during the Jesus Movement of the '60s and '70s. I didn't know the songs but did my best to follow along. Moved by the music, a feeling of peace came and the presence of an unknown spirit. My friend explained it was the Holy Ghost. I could feel love in the music and craved more.

**Moved by the music, a feeling of peace came and the presence of an unknown spirit.**

As I've mentioned, music is an instrumental part of my perspective in life. It's a powerful tool for change in cultures and individuals. Bob Dylan's song "The Times They Are a-Changin'" is a classic example. That song holds true to me today just as it did in the '60s. It makes sense the songs at church would catalyze an important change in my life.

I returned to church the next week to learn more about the Holy Ghost. The worship music evoked peace and comfort. Afterward, the pastor read from the Gospel of John:

"There was a man named Nicodemus, a Jewish religious leader who was a Pharisee. After dark one evening, he came to speak with Jesus. 'Rabbi,' he said, 'we all know that God has sent you to teach us. Your miraculous signs are evidence that God is with you.'

Jesus replied, 'I tell you the truth, unless you are born again, you cannot see the Kingdom of God.'

'What do you mean?' exclaimed Nicodemus. 'How can an old man go back into his mother's womb and be born again?'

Jesus replied, 'I assure you; no one can enter the Kingdom of God without being born of water and the Spirit.'"

The pastor said it was paramount to be filled with the Holy Ghost and that the Holy Ghost gives power. As a truth seeker, this appealed to me. After service I introduced myself to him and asked how to be filled with the Spirit.

"All you have to do is ask," he said.

I admitted my lifestyle was a mess. He prayed for me and for my salvation, but I wasn't sure if I was born again. *Should I feel different? Do I need to do something?* He was kind, patient, and loving when he said, "Mark it's not what *you* do. Jesus already paid the price. It's a gift."

"But how do I know for sure?"

He chuckled and said, "You get filled with the Holy Ghost and will know for certain."

Not feeling any different after more prayer, I asked, "How will it affect me?"

He then read from the book of Acts: "And they were all filled with the Holy Ghost and began to speak with other tongues, as the Spirit gave them utterance."

We prayed some more. Still nothing. Frustrated, I went home but returned for the evening service. A Messianic Jew preached from both the Old and New Testament as a guest speaker that night, and afterward, he asked if anyone wanted to be baptized by the Holy Ghost. I stepped forward and was encircled by young believers in Christ. He placed his hands on my head and prayed for me. Within minutes, an overwhelming sense of God's Spirit flowed from the top of my head down through my spine and to my toes. My hands lifted, and I started speaking gibberish, or rather, tongues. I was praising the Creator of the universe and didn't want to stop. The visiting pastor told me to continue speaking my heavenly language. I was unspeakably joyful—as soon as I got home, I threw away all my drugs and paraphernalia.

> **As soon as I got home, I threw away all my drugs and paraphernalia.**

For the first time in my life I felt clean. The high I felt from God was better than any drug, traveling adventure, ski run, rock concert, or party I'd ever experienced. That night, I fell asleep speaking in tongues, woke up in the middle of the night speaking some more. In the morning I started again—unlike taking drugs or alcohol, when I awoke with a hangover, I was still high and full of joy. Jesus filled me and changed my life forever, transforming a poor, addicted druggie into a respected, successful, family man.

> **For the first time in my life I felt clean.**

God's constant love, patience, and guiding the Holy Spirit are my salvation. Today, my wife and I are elders in our church and involved with helping others find their purpose in life.

"Create in me a clean heart, O God, And renew a right and steadfast spirit within me." —Psalm 51:10

## Rhonda Castanon, author, entrepreneur

Author Rhonda Castanon has always been willing and driven to step into the challenging places of people's lives. Rhonda worked tirelessly with the Florida State Attorney's Office as a victim rights advocate and volunteered with Pinellas and Orange counties as a Guardian Ad Litem for children. As a domestic violence advocate, she educated and trained various law enforcement personnel, court officials, minors, and adults in school, halfway houses, and jails, as well as spearheaded and participated in ground-breaking programs.

Christ eventually led Rhonda to open her own law firm, conduct estate planning seminars, and air-dropped a golden opportunity to take an unprecedented leap of growth in her career. Then, everything turned upside down and Christ rebuilt her into the spiritual warrior He needed her to become so she was ready for the future He had for her.

In her book, *Journey Derailed: Is Your Hope for Healing Tied to a Diagnosis, an Expected Outcome, a Cure, or to Christ?*, Rhonda tells her almost two-decade journey of unimaginable suffering from an unexpected chronic illness, leading to the dissolution of her law firm and career. Plunged into a darkness she thought she would never rise above, Christ took her on a most unexpected route resulting in startling breakthroughs and renewal.

Living in Clermont, Florida, Rhonda is a wife to a retired firefighter, a mother of two young-adult children, and a Kingdom entrepreneur for her Lord and Savior Jesus Christ.

To find out more about Rhonda, please visit:
**www.JourneyDerailed.com**
or on Facebook and Instagram: @journeyderailed

## CHAPTER EIGHT
## Rhonda Castanon

# BUT, LORD...THAT'S ABSURD!

*So this is why people commit suicide*—the thought struck me with the force of a lightning bolt and with the same instantaneous flash of illumination. It wasn't a question to myself as much as a statement, like the slow dawning of divine insight that dropped like a bomb into the idyllic scene unfolding before my eyes. My six-year-old son, Zack, and my five-year-old daughter, Kaylee, were racing all over our backyard playing superhero tag. Both kids were donned only in capes, underwear, and shoes—super shoes to protect against spiders, scorpions, and snakes, oh my!

My dynamic duo, with their capes flapping, were loving life. The capes, which held the mystery to their superpowers, were cut out of those old, soft, fleece-type infant blankets every parent owns.

Kaylee squealed with delight as her beloved big brother chased her around our backyard and purposely never quite caught up to her. I heard the pure, unfiltered joy projected out of my child's laughter— a unique sound owned only by children. This living sound radiating deep from within them washed over me and surrounded my soul. My heart swelled with love for them then pinched like a vise because I was not out there running around and acting silly right along with them. Instead, I was in my bedroom, filled with a mix of anger, sadness, confusion, and hopelessness.

Abruptly, I felt slammed back into my own pain-riddled body and my reality screamed once more at me. *How is this my life? How can I keep making it through each day when all I want to do is peel my skin off!* Once again, I'm in bed, desperately willing my pain and my sheer exhaustion to be something other than utterly excruciating, depleting, and mind numbing.

*You can do this Rhonda; put your hand down on the bed and push up!* roared inside my own head. I fruitlessly demanded my body and mind to cooperate and find a way to engage with my kids. My soul felt crushed. Through gritted teeth, I practically spit out the words, "I do not want my children's memory of me to be as an invalid who's always in bed." The ferocity of my own emotions frightened me.

Startled by splashes of water hitting my hand, I was suddenly aware of the tears cascading down my face. My whole body seemed incoherently detached from my conscious brain. *How can I stay reliant on You, Jesus, when I can barely comprehend how to survive the next minute of this pain? What am I supposed to do, Lord?* I pleaded for the umpteenth time.

> **The ferocity of my own emotions frightened me.**

This moment was a turning point, a foreshadowing of only *one* of Christ's many purposes behind homeschooling—to redirect my focus outside of myself, my pain, onto a positive and fulfilling reason to force myself out of bed every day. In 2003, just a few short years prior to this rude awakening, I suddenly began experiencing 24/7 migraines which led to 24/7 severe pain from the top of my head to the tips of my toes.

From 2003 until I first launched our little homeschool experiment in 2007, a lot had happened to me. I had closed my law practice and was forced to walk away from an "only God can do that" golden opportunity to succeed my legal mentor's practice upon her near retirement. I closed my law practice and transferred to a large firm hoping to reduce my stress and pain and protect my clients. Shortly after that transfer, I discovered my headaches were caused by two cervical vertebrae grinding on each other. So, I underwent a cervical fusion surgery, and then we moved to a remote area of a new city for the remainder of my recovery without knowing if I'd ever return to the legal profession. At the time, I was in my early 30's, married to a firefighter, and had two young children.

The surgery stopped the headaches but did not touch the severe, chronic pain consuming my body, mind, and soul. Unbeknownst to me, I was only just beginning my search for answers to my mysterious health issues and my experimentation with countless naturopathic protocols, experiments with diets and detox "solutions," non-traditional practices far beyond just acupuncture and massage, as well as traditional medical approaches and specialists galore.

To say my life felt wrecked would be an understatement. *Why on earth would I homeschool and how's it even possible with all I'm going through?* Christ made it crystal clear; He had been dropping homeschooling seeds into my life even before my health declined, but I wasn't listening. His baby steps for me started with discussions between my husband, Al, and I when we were first trying to have a child and how we would handle daycare.

> **To say my life felt wrecked would be an understatement.**

These discussions led to Al and me co-sharing baby duty—I stayed home and worked remotely on the two days a week Al had his 24-hour shift. This arrangement opened my mind to the joy and privilege of parenting and to never allow work to overshadow family life. Before getting married, all I ever wanted was a career. To me, the family/kid stuff just came…later, after the established career.

With that kind of mindset, clearly homeschooling was not even a possible blip on my life's radar. In fact, I had never even heard about homeschooling until I met all these stay-at-home moms who taught their own kids in our Orlando church. *Great for them, but I can't homeschool while continuing with a career.* So, yes, you guessed it, I dismissed such a silly notion. *It's just not possible, not realistic.*

Christ watered the little homeschooling seeds He was dropping into our lives when Kaylee couldn't transfer to a new VPK (Voluntary Pre-Kindergarten) program in Clermont. She missed the age cutoff to start Kindergarten in the new public elementary school, so she now had to be home with me. *Well, isn't that convenient.* With the advice and guidance of the wonderful ladies from my Orlando church, I did 30 minutes to an hour each day of fundamental cognitive, motor, and reading skills aimed at preparing her for public school. The following school year, I registered both kids at the local public elementary school.

Then, Christ decided to kick things up a notch. Mind you, in the interim, ping-ponging back and forth between Al and myself was this wavering sense of conviction we should homeschool. Al would agree, but I would falter, then vice versa. Finally, He just deluged me with water to wake me up. He used the women's Bible study group I joined as His final "powering up" move to get my attention.

We were studying *Lies Women Believe and the Truth that Sets Them Free* by Nancy Leigh DeMoss. One of the chapters was about having and raising children. As I read the chapter, I realized I had never thought to ask God about when to have kids, how many, or anything.

Through the discussion and answering the chapter questions, Christ used a Thor-sized sledgehammer to pound home His message to me: "You will homeschool your kids. Period. End of story. Stop procrastinating." Just like that, I knew I *was* procrastinating. I knew what Christ laid on my heart. I knew Al sensed it, too. We were afraid to face that truth because…well, it seemed absurd.

I left the Bible study and immediately wrote out a multi-page letter to Al. Christ opened my eyes and my soul and everything inside me flooded onto those pages. Tears freely flowed, obscuring my ability to see well enough to keep writing. Christ downloaded the words to me. Every thought, feeling, and sentence seemed to simply ooze out of my pen, functioning almost like a chemical reaction, materializing invisible ink onto my paper. In total abandonment, He revealed things to me I didn't even realize I was ignoring or feeling until I wrote out that letter.

My prayer had been for Al to not just agree to homeschool but to truly *want* to homeschool—for us to be united in the decision. Christ answered my prayer through that letter. Those Spirit-inspired words pierced straight into Al's heart. In Al's beautiful way, he gushed out how he knew too but was concerned about a negative impact on my health.

Even after the dramatic way Christ got my attention, I still brazenly told the Lord He was crazy to think I could handle any degree of structure or mental exertion. I remember sitting with the Lord and outlining all the reasons I needed a simple, pre-boxed, preplanned, just point and teach type curriculum. *I can see how it might work but not if I have to put everything together. You know what my days are like, what my brain is like. I can hang up the phone and not just forget who I was speaking to and what we spoke about but even that I had the call at all. I want to peel my skin off my body every day. Sitting hurts. Thinking hurts. My existence hurts. Homeschooling…it's just crazy, but I'll do it. You made it clear, but it's just not realistic unless it's as simple and straightforward for me as possible.* I wonder if Jesus ever does eye rolls?

While I was busy researching my best pre-designed curriculum, Christ opened up another door: the Charlotte Mason Method. My friend, Michelle, who also homeschooled, told me all about this young British woman and her teaching tenets. She felt the words I used to express what I hoped to do for my kids in this new venture were perfectly matched with what Charlotte's style was all about. However, it was not a "ready-made" method, she told me.

Intrigued, I began to read about this most remarkable woman. Michelle was right; it wasn't pre-packaged, but it spoke to the deepest part of my soul. Charlotte believed "education was an atmosphere, a discipline, and a life; it was about finding out who we were and how we fit into the world of human beings and into the universe God created." Education was defined as "a series of relationships formed by the learner as he developed intimacy with a wide range of subjects," which she referred to as "the science of relations."

I agreed with her that children should directly "deal with ideas and knowledge that they are not blank slates or empty sacks to be filled with information." There was such intention behind every core teaching tenet, and I wanted my children to have the experience with learning she described. At the time, these teaching tenets spoke to me only because I saw the value for my kids.

Much later, Christ revealed to me how He wielded these methods as weapons to help me navigate the pain—I'll get to those gems in a bit. At this point, Christ used Charlotte Mason to stir my soul and confirm this was the path for our homeschooling; it terrified me. *How am I supposed to do this, Lord?*

I felt woefully unprepared to tackle the concentration, reading, learning curve, and time necessary to implement these methods. This is precisely what I had told the Lord—that I couldn't possibly homeschool this way. But, in the middle of all my anger and confusion, in all the uncertainty and unknowns, we started our little Wings Like Eagles Academy for the

**How am I supposed to do this, Lord? I feel woefully unprepared.**

2007-2008 school year. Kaylee was in first grade and Zack was in third grade.

I'm not going to lie, it was tough—almost brutal at times; physically, mentally, and emotionally—but teaching also brought me unbelievable, true joy. Yes, the pain was ever present and ever oppressive. Pure faith and Christ's strength alone allowed me to accomplish the monumental task of teaching. I taught at the picnic table Al built for us on our back patio, while lying in bed, and sitting on the couch. In the beginning, my goal for teaching was a maximum of two hours a day.

Many times, I divided up those hours as opposed to continuing consecutively. The kids worked on other homework, projects, and reading when I wasn't teaching. Al pitched in as well. I even relied on Zack to handle some of the reading normally assigned to me when my eyes couldn't focus well enough or my mind couldn't stay alert. We didn't read grade level or simple books either, so the Lord really blessed me through my son because he was such a strong reader.

We went outside and explored nature every day. We used our nature journals to draw pictures of or simply name various plants, insects, spiders, flowers, birds, and other animals we discovered on our outings together. The kids then had to write some of the scientific classifications or habitat information for any critter.

Our subdivision backed up to woods and an old orange grove, so we saw all varieties of birds including hawks, falcons, turkey vultures, guinea hens, and woodpeckers, as well as pygmy rattlers, turtles, tortoises, fox, bobcats, wild boar, deer, otters, and alligators, to name a few of the larger species. We read books in the trees. We made up dance movements to Bach and experimented with the painting techniques of Kahlo, Picasso, Pollack, and Van Gogh.

If not for these things, I would've been lying lifelessly in my bed, moping, feeling sorry for myself. When every millimeter of my skin, muscle, and bone seethed with pain, why would I *want* to move, causing even more pain, unless really motivated? The Lord knew what He was doing by leading us to a teaching method that allowed us such simple joys and connection with one another.

As soon as I completed teaching each day, my whole body visibly shook, vibration-like, due to the energy I expended struggling through our lesson time. One day, all I could accomplish afterward was taking one or two bites of an apple and a small block of cheese I'd grabbed while beelining for the spare bedroom. Immediately, I put my food down and collapsed into the bed in a bizarre half-awake state. It was like sleep paralysis—I could hear but I couldn't move, not without extreme mental gymnastics to will my physical body into compliance.

Christ knew how difficult this task would be even in 100 percent perfect health, let alone while battling against the infamous four-star general, General Pain, and all his minions. Christ knew I needed powerful motivation in my life to prevail against the relentless onslaught of pain, doubt, self-pity, despondency, despair, exhaustion, indignation, and fear. Guided demon-arrows of destruction were strategically aimed at puncturing every millimeter of my body and my mind to deflate God's purpose for me and to send me retreating from Christ's call.

What was Christ's grand strategy? He wielded homeschooling into a shield of joy for me—a weapon to deflect this intended rain of death by a thousand cuts.

> **Christ weaponized me.**

*Homeschooling as a battle strategy…odd, curious.* However, I still had the pain. Christ didn't remove my physical misery; instead He weaponized me. He was incentivizing me to keep fighting by witnessing the wonder of life through my children's eyes, returning me to all the things I enjoyed as a kid, and by showing up and showing off in our lives.

I was awestruck at how insightful, smart, and quick to learn my children were about so many things. I felt tingly all over when one of God's many gemstone moments with my kids caused me to reflect, *Wow, I would have missed this if I still worked.* These were moments which existed only because my kids and I had daily, simple, random conversations about everything and nothing, all at the same time.

Every time life started tipping upside down, the kids would make me laugh or make a spontaneous connection, improve in recall ability, or discover another unnamed flower, plant, or bug. When this happened, all other angst melted away. The amount of time all four of us spent together as a family was another priceless jewel from Christ. The number of places we traveled to, as well as the types of things Al and I were able to do with the kids for educational purposes and just for fun, was staggering and forged a strong family bond; a bond the pain could've easily ripped apart.

Homeschooling nurtured me with fond memories from my own childhood, like how much I always loved to read, to explore, and to learn. I was listening to rich, wonderful stories with my children that vividly described all areas of world history, science, and classic literature. More than bringing joy and childhood reflections, our homeschooling methods were surreptitiously helping me in tangible ways.

The way we homeschooled further saturated me in the Word of God. We read directly from the Bible, and all school topics were discussed through the biblical prism. We discovered how much history and science simply confirmed what God's Word says about planets, orbits, the body, and nature. I learned church history, world history and biblical history as an integrated timeline. Suddenly, I'm seeing God's hand in everything and connecting Scripture, current world events, and biblical history into a cohesive whole that further deepened and opened my understanding of all of those same categories.

As my Bible knowledge and spiritual understanding grew, I witnessed God moving in our lives in real time, answering prayers and guiding us through each school year. Charlotte's beliefs in reading smaller chunks in lots of high-quality books with an emphasis on games and tactile manipulation for math slowly improved my recall and retention capabilities. Reading the missionary book series *Christian Heroes: Then and Now* encouraged my belief that God could do for me what He did for so many other ordinary people faced with seemingly insurmountable problems. Even one of our writing programs was directly responsible for transforming my writing skills, thereby increasing my desire to write again.

All these details show how well Christ knows me. Christ knew I needed to feel useful. I was still a wife and mother regardless of what my body, mind, and soul felt like every day. Christ knew I needed focus and a positive distraction which awakened a purpose-driven life within me. He knew my body and soul needed nourishment to withstand what the pain was attempting to take from me, giving me hope that I still had a future. Now, Christ is using all I went through to write books and share the many lessons learned with others.

I prayed for relief from the pain. Christ counterattacked the pain with something that would allow me to grow into the spiritual warrior I needed to become. Why? I believe it was not just to help me endure unimaginable pain or for my family. Christ wanted to demonstrate that my expectations for how He should

> **Christ knew I needed focus and a positive distraction which awakened a purpose-driven life within me.**

answer my prayers sabotaged my faith in His ability to resolve what I can't figure out. He works in mysterious ways, and I needed to allow Him to work however He wants. I had to be willing to step past my own limitations and allow Christ to provide unexpected divine provision disguised as an impossible task presented at the worst possible time!

If He can put an unexpected gift in my life—an unusual weapon for victory—He can do it for you, too, if you allow it. Watch for it!

## Joelene Powell,
### author, mentor, creative

Author Joelene Powell has walked with the Lord 38 years. Joelene is a single mother of three amazing, young-adult boys and has recently gained the status of GiGi to twins who are also amazing. As a friend and mentor to many, she also loves serving her community in various ways.

Professionally, Joelene has been in healthcare for over 26 years. She is an adjunct professor who has taught, created, and developed courses and curriculum for the past 13 years.

Joelene's heart is for singing and writing. She now leads the Ozarks Chapter of the Kingdom Writer's Association. She is a leader who is passionate about people developing a more intimate relationship and walking with the Father. The One who held her walked with her and has been her rock/refuge in the darkest times throughout the years.

To learn more about Joelene, please visit:

**JoPowell.my.canva.site**

# Hidden Things Healed by the Light

The mirror is our best and worst friend, and yet we keep returning time and time again. If a friend treated you like the mirror, you would no longer be friends. You would walk away from the toxicity of the relationship. What if the words the mirror or others had to say didn't cut so deep? What if it didn't matter at all? What if your identity came from above? What if you were meant for more? What if you have been called to be set apart…to be different? What if God had an authentic purpose and plan specifically for you? Would you be willing to let go of the anger, hurt, fear, bitterness, and pain of the past long enough to find out?

If you said yes, I invite you to journey with me through this chapter. I will attempt to share my story and answer those questions and more. I pray you realize how instead of relying on the mirror or others, we get to embrace being seen through the eyes of the Father.

*The darkness of the night is too quiet. My mind won't quit thinking about the events of the day. I can't sleep, so I decide to seek the one thing that I think will help. I sneak into the kitchen, open the freezer, and see what I am seeking. It is better than any prize to me at this moment. There is no judgment. It doesn't talk back, and oh how wonderful it tastes.*

*Without a sound, I grab two and then tiptoe down the hallway to the bathroom, ever so careful to not make any noise. I don't even turn on the light for fear of being found out. I quietly close the door, praying it doesn't creak, and lock it. Then, I walk over to the toilet, put the lid down, and sit. The seat's cold, but I don't care. Unwrapping my first gift to myself, I revel in its three rich and creamy flavors. I don't know how I even know it tastes good because I inhale it so quickly. It is gone in seconds. Then, on to the next. This one is the same amazing chocolate, vanilla, and strawberry with a cookie outside…gone within seconds.*

*My joy is fleeting. I can't risk being seen or found out. I don't dare risk throwing up for fear someone will hear. I hate throwing up anyway! Believe me, I have tried several times.*

This began a cycle of eating and hiding. Two soon became three, which turned into four, and so on. Sweets were my drug of choice—my attempt to try to heal all the emotions running wild in my mind. No one ever knew. I'm not even sure they suspected. I was great at hiding and replacing.

Family is what everyone strives to have in life. It is amazing, beautiful, and even supportive when it works. When it doesn't, it can break you. The hurt and pain cut so deep it's almost paralyzing. Growing up, I always heard you can choose your friends, not your family. This is so true. For as long as I can remember, until my grandmother could no longer host them, my family would gather for Sunday dinner after church—kids at the smaller table, adults at the big table. There were a bunch of us. It was always my uncle and his family, Grandma, Grandpa, and my parents, along with my sisters and brothers. Some Sundays we would have extended family or the pastor would join us. It was a time of laughing, playing, talking, and coming of age...until it shifted.

The family always prayed first, then began to eat and talk. The activity in the kitchen could be intense. Every Sunday, I can remember from a young age, my uncle would make rude comments to my aunt. He didn't care who was at the table or who was visiting. Sunday after Sunday he would put down her weight. He would say things like, "Hey, blimpo," or "Hey, lardo." She would try to laugh it off, but I could see the pain his words caused her.

My uncle was not a mean man by any means, and for anyone who knew him, this was completely out of character. Yet somehow, treating others in this manner was okay with him. I will never forget the day his attention turned to *me*. We were at Grandma's Sunday dinner, and I had just come in. He said, "Hey, Jolie Blonde, you are getting a little thick, aren't you?" I was in shock. I didn't know what to even say. I felt as if someone had knocked the wind out of me. Tears threatened to come. They were just at the edge of my eyes,

> **I felt as if someone had knocked the wind out of me.**

but I held them back. I didn't dare let anyone see the effect that his comment had. Everyone sat there. *No one* said a word. My dad said nothing. My mom said nothing. No one stood up for me! The room was silent. They just let him say it. I felt alone. I felt betrayed. I felt as if all the security and safety I was supposed to have evaporated into thin air.

That Sunday marked the beginning of a cycle of emotional abuse that continued from about fourth grade until I left for college. A constant stream of nasty insults awaited me. When I walked into the kitchen on any given Sunday, I never knew what was going to happen. Looking back, it reminds me of when I try to go to the carwash after a snowstorm. You know, when cars line up as far as the eye can see? It was like that—a revolving door of insults with no end in sight. That was my life for more than ten years.

I would hear, "Jolie Blonde, you are getting fatter." "Jolie Blonde, do you think you need to be eating that?" "Jolie Blonde! Did you lose weight?" "Jolie Blonde, my you sure are a thick one!" One Sunday after dinner, while we girls were doing dishes, a comment was made, "Oh, that's just your uncle." At least someone finally acknowledged it, right? I hated Sunday dinners.

With each passing week, the words played over and over in my mind. They settled in my thoughts. They took root in my heart. They festered. It wasn't long before I allowed the pain, anger, and bitterness to eat away at me. Instead of lashing out at others, I turned on myself with negative self-talk. I believed those lies he had spoken over me. I hated myself and lost sight of who I was. Finding solace in food and emotionally eating, I became an epic binge eater. I learned how to hide food. Thus began the late-night bathroom escapades. The sweeter the food, and if it was packaged, the better.

> **Instead of lashing out at others, I turned on myself with negative self-talk.**

From ages 11-16, I babysat for several families. It was a joy because I adored kids and had the best clients. Those families would refer me to their friends for even more babysitting jobs because they loved having me. Not only did I watch their children, but I would clean their homes, too.

I tell you this not to brag, but simply to share more of the story. It's amazing what can happen behind closed doors—things no one knows about. There was a dark secret behind the reason I was cleaning all the houses. I felt guilty because I loved watching their children. I played with them and did anything else that needed to be done before bedtime. Then, as soon as the children went to bed, I would head to the pantry. If there wasn't a pantry, I would head to the cupboards.

Besides babysitting, my other skill was knowing how to take just enough food and rearrange the cabinet or pantry so no one could tell anything was missing. Oh, my goodness…the food I ate! Looking back on it is alarming. I sat on the floor. I tore into item after item, cramming one thing in after another. Inhaling it as fast as I could. Barely breathing. Barely tasting. The high came from sneaking the food. And from the sugar. It was the high of how much I could eat without being caught.

I remember house-sitting at a condo one time. The pantry was enormous and filled to the top. I had my pick of anything. I pulled out every snack and junk food item I could grab without it being noticeable that it was missing. It was glorious. Doughnuts, candy bars, crackers, snack cakes. You name it; I found it. I had to be quick. I had a rough estimate of when the parents would be back.

I sat in the middle of the pantry floor, hiding. Then, I would cram in as much as I could. There was no judgment here. No one laughing at me. No one telling me I couldn't eat this or that. No one telling me how pretty I would be if I only stayed this exact size. I would eat until I was so stuffed I wanted to vomit. I would eat until all the hurt seemed a little less. I would eat until I stopped remembering and just concentrated on the food in front of me.

The enemy would tell me food was my friend. Food was my escape. There was no judgment in food. Food would take all my cares away and make me feel better. The enemy used those lies so often. Although my stomach would ache, I would just keep going until everything in front of me was gone.

As soon as I finished, I would scrub and clean the kitchen from top to bottom and take out the trash, leaving no evidence. Then, I would vacuum the entire house, even clean the bathrooms so as not to look suspicious. I became a well-paid, highly recommended babysitter with a very sad, dark secret. I was a closet binge eater who was completely out of control, yet it spiraled down even more.

Instead of just occasionally binging during babysitting, I was binge eating three to four times a week. I had been sick as a child, so it was easy to stay home from school and binge eat if I chose. I opted to do so as often as possible, because why not? I didn't have many friends anyway; no one liked me because of my weight (and an embarrassing situation with a see-through swimsuit). So, why bother going to school? Seclusion and isolation became my allies. I learned to have a few friends, but also to keep them at arm's length so I wouldn't get hurt again.

In eighth grade, I decided I was going on a major diet. Not just *any* diet—a pure liquid diet for the entire summer. I lost 50 pounds. This was the unhealthiest thing, and yet everyone told me how amazing I looked. I was told if I could just stay this size, I would be "perfect." I was in a constant state of binge eating and dieting—a recurring cycle that had taken over my life. In the fourth grade I started dieting and had tried every diet in the book.

By this time, I had developed body dysmorphia. I could not see what was real, not even if I tried—not even if I could hear God, which was not happening at that time. Every time I looked into the mirror, all I saw was an obese "lardo" with rolls and rolls of fat that no one would ever love or want. The mind is a curious thing. I could keep the reels of negative self-talk going, and what my uncle had spoken over me kept replaying for years!

During my first year of college, I was able to stabilize my eating and find peace with myself. Feeling content and being away from home, the binge eating ceased.

> **I could not see what was real, not even if I tried.**

There were no more Sunday dinners. There was no judgment. For the first time in years, I was free from being reminded every minute of my weight.

The following year, I married my high-school sweetheart. As a new bride, I had such high hopes and fairy-tale dreams. You fall in love and get married. Your husband loves you for who you are, and you live happily ever after. That's what my generation was taught as children.

Sadly, that was not to be the case. One day, while I was making dinner, my husband looked me up and down and said, "Don't worry about your size. You will lose it after you have kids." It was like he dumped a bucket of ice water on me. All the childhood emotions and images came flooding back. I felt ashamed. I felt guilty. My body was not what he wanted. It needed to change.

This was an instant trigger for me, and it sent me into a new spiral. This one was even more intense than before. I drove through fast-food restaurants on the way home from work and gorged myself. I could put away many candy bars at a time. Prior to this, my dieting was about changing food habits. Now, I became extreme. I joined diet programs. I started researching and taking over-the-counter and prescription pills, laxatives, and eventually, tried to induce vomiting.

One of my lowest points was the beta HCG diet in my mid-twenties. I was eating less than 500 calories a day…basically starving my body! It did marvelous things for my body, according to my coach. But then I developed gallstones (which was a side-effect of the diet) and had to undergo surgery. That was the end of the beta HCG diet.

After almost 15 years into our marriage and three children later, my husband sat me down one evening. He told me he didn't love me anymore and that he never wanted to be married. He wanted to be sure I knew it was never because of my weight. This is another story. But did you catch the last part? "I'm not leaving you because of your weight!" My heart felt crushed—like someone took a sledgehammer, placed my heart on a railroad tie, and smashed it. My best friend, the love of my life, just denounced all that I knew. He crushed what little self-worth I had left. Or did he?

One year to the day prior to this, God led me to take a faith walk.

He gave me a verse: *"Trust in the LORD with all your heart and lean not on your own understanding; In all your ways acknowledge Him, and He shall direct your paths"* ( Proverbs 3:5-6).

For that entire year, I was in the Word and living in a constant state of praise and worship. This is all that was keeping the fragments of my heart from completely shattering. I thought the year was preparation for something else, but God saw the bigger picture. Thankfully, I had postured my heart to hear His voice. After that gut-wrenching night, I was determined to get myself mentally, physically, and spiritually healthy for my children. That sounds like the right idea, doesn't it? And yet, the motivation of your children (or any other human) can only sustain you for so long before you cycle back into old habits. And cycle I did.

> **Thankfully, I had postured my heart to hear His voice.**

I was taking off weight. I was putting weight on. Weighing myself every morning and every night. Laxatives in the morning and at night, if needed. Only protein liquid at night if weighing in. I had it down to an art, if there is such a thing. What I learned was that pushing something down and hiding it in the deep crevices of my mind and heart only caused the pressure to build. At some point, the pressure must be released.

I would love to tell you the road to breakthrough happened all at once and overnight. Sadly, it did not. My journey was and is just that: a journey. I would do well for a bit and then cycle back into old habits. Although I never turned my back on God, I drifted away from listening to His voice and staying in alignment with Him at times. I would get close, do better, and think *I've got this*. Then, when I failed, I would run back to the Father.

At some point though, something shifted within me! The Father is where I finally found my identity. I learned I am the daughter of the Creator, made in His image. I believed I mattered. I liked myself— something I had never said before. He had made beauty from ashes. I believed I was His original prototype. He made me unique and gifted me for such a time as this.

My heart transformed to where I could see the hand of God all over my life. I could see the grace that He had given me. Daily, I began studying the Word and started each day in praise and worship. I sang and lifted my voice to Him all day long. I spoke positive declarations over my life of who I am and *whose* I am. The negative self-talk was leaving me. I began eliminating negative people from my life. The footprints of God were visible everywhere I went.

God showed me there is breakthrough in trusting in the fullness of His love. The Father showed me He did not make a mistake; I was not a mistake. He showed me the lies of the enemy and the years Satan had robbed me of my joy, my peace, my dance, and my happiness. Father showed me He would redeem all that had been lost. He showed me a better way. He opened my eyes to see what was truly in the mirror for the first time in nearly 40 years of life.

**There is breakthrough in trusting in the fullness of His love.**

Are there times when I have the urge to revert? Absolutely. Are there times I have stumbled? Yes, and yet I still know whose I am. In those moments, I hear the Father say, "Is that of Me?" Then, I take a step back and refocus. Looking to Him to see my identity has changed my perspective. Looking to Him to gauge my reaction to emotions has helped me to refocus and take my mind off of food. I renewed my mind to put my thoughts in the right order to let the Father be my guide in all things.

God has done exceedingly more than I can ask in my life. My uncle passed away several years ago from dementia. On one last visit, something amazing happened that I will never forget. I saw the fog lift from his eyes as he was entering the house. He looked me straight in the eyes and said, "I owe you an apology, don't I? For several things?" I said, "Yes, you do!" He said, "I'm sorry." Then his eyes clouded back over in the next instant, as if nothing happened. This was a gift from the Father. At that moment, I needed that apology. I needed closure. I needed life to come full circle.

The road may not always be easy. Yet, the Father is here, and just like He was waiting for my *yes*, He is waiting for yours. He is waiting to help you, too. The Father wants you to know He sees you, all of you! Even those things you have hidden in secret, just as I did. The time has come to let them go. It's time to be free! It is time to trust that the Father loves you so much and He can handle *anything*. It's time to touch the hem of His garment and receive wholeness! He can take what's fragmented in us and restore it to beauty. He showed me a healthier way to live, and I am working to walk in that way every day—not only for myself, but for my children and their children as well.

"He has made everything beautiful in its time."
—Ecclesiastes 3:11a

## Desireé Theassa Young,
### Author, Speaker, Singer

Desireé holds a BA in psychology from Carthage College where she double minored in creative writing and Japanese. She is a chapter leader for Kingdom Writers Association in Waukesha, WI, a resource center dedicated to empowering and encouraging Christian writers of all levels to follow their calling.

Desireé finished writing her first book during quarantine in 2020 and has not slowed down. She continues to write and also takes speaking engagements to educate people about human trafficking, which is the subject of her first book, *Kaleidoscope: A Journey to Hope.*

Following one of her biggest passions, Desireé formed Glory Cloud Resting in 2022. Glory Cloud Resting is a group of creatives who bring people into an encounter with God through words and music. Their first album, *Come to Glory,* comes out in the summer of 2023 along with a devotional. Get a sneak peek on Glory Cloud Resting's YouTube channel.

In 2023, Desiree launched a clothing collection called R.I.S.E— Remember I'm Strong Enough. This clothing collection has a simple yet powerful message, and has evolved to include online courses on a variety of topics such as forgiveness, identity, and an abundant life. There's also a course for adults who came from divorced parents called Exchanging Pain for Love.

In her free time, Desireé enjoys hiking, dancing, photography, looking for sea glass, superhero shows and movies, and spending time with her loved ones. She currently resides in Menomonee Falls, WI.

Writings: www.TheVaultOfTheScribe.com
Ministry: www.RiseMinistries413.com
Music: youtube.com/@glorycloudresting

Learn more at:

**www.TheVaultOfTheScribe.com**

# CHAPTER TEN
## Desiree T. Young

# From Child of Pain to Child of Love

No parent wants to have or contribute to an unhealthy environment for their kids. Most parents, when they hold their baby girl or boy for the first time, dream of giving them the world. Even so, what they dream and what becomes reality can sometimes be different. Growing up, there were good things that occurred in my parents' home. My dad established several family traditions that I look forward to doing with my own kids someday—things like taking family trips to D.C. and Ocean City and having family game nights. These are memories I look back on with joy and gratitude. They are beautiful moments I will carry with me forever. But for each of these happy memories, there are several that broke my heart.

I grew up a child of divorce. My parents split when I was still in diapers, and I grew up living at both houses. Both of them remarried, but each of those marriages also had an expiration date. The second divorce occurred when I was in elementary school. My stepmother at the time was angry and chose to make life difficult for my dad because he was fighting for full custody of my youngest brother. Her lies and deception got him put in jail for 24 hours, and my aunt had to get me from school. Seeing my dad as the target of her venom was awful. *How could someone go from loving and sharing their life with someone else to trying to destroy them so easily? Did she ever love him at all?* When all was said and done, the judge gave my father full custody and she was out of our lives. Years went by. Then one day out of blue, she called, announcing her name as if we were waiting with baited breath for her. I told her she had the wrong number and hung up.

Divorce number three came out of nowhere. It was late in my high school years, and I remember the day Mom asked my stepdad to leave. I couldn't understand it. *Where was he going? And why?* This family of ours wasn't perfect, but it worked. A mom who was kind,

99

compassionate, and gracious—the one who always encouraged me to sing, play piano, and voluntold me to do church plays. A dad who works hard and teaches us about integrity and striving for excellence—the man I credit for my unashamed obsession with superheroes, the one who got my brother into sports he really enjoyed. *Where is he going?* I listened at the top of the stairs while they were arguing. This safe and secure home was coming apart, and there was nothing I could do to stop it. I was helpless. *Is love a lie? Till death do us part... Are those just empty words?* All I could do was hug my brother and tell him everything was going to be okay, even though I didn't know how.

> **Is love a lie?**

My dad and second stepmom's marriage had many problems that they both contributed to. They fought every day, multiple times a day—even on Christmas. There was no peace, and laughter was fleeting. I remember hearing my stepmom plead with Dad over the phone on a number of occasions to come home from the casino. She just wanted to spend time with him. I could hear her crying alone in her room, heartbroken that he'd said no. She had a love language of quality time, but found rejection when trying to do activities with him. Hearing and seeing her pain made me sad. I wished I could make it better. *What if I called? Would Dad come home then?* I never tried, but always wondered.

My stepmom was just very unhappy. She blamed everyone and everything else for it—where she lived, her kids, her husband, her finances. The dogs were the only constant good thing. When I tried to do chores, I was yelled at for not doing them correctly. I used too much soap when cleaning the dishes. After a while, I stopped trying. I often slept late on the weekends and my waking up at noon irritated her. My morning shower took ten minutes, and that was too long. I liked to sing, but my voice was irritating to my dad and stepmom. Often, I was told to shut up. According to my dad, whenever they argued it was about *me*. I was responsible for their unhappiness. He told me this when I told him I didn't want to spend the night at his house anymore; I was a junior in high school. All the arguing had pushed me to my breaking point. It was overwhelming me, and I couldn't take it anymore.

At the time, I believed it *was* my fault. Looking back now, I see that it wasn't. I hadn't heard the arguments they had about me. I did hear the ones they had about my brother, their finances, household contributions, the dogs, and their finances some more. I prayed for them for years, even giving them resources on how to improve their marriage. I spent time fasting for them, just hoping they would reconcile. They went to marriage counseling for a little while, and it helped. But soon they stopped going and the toxicity came back full force.

I entered college broken-hearted and broken-spirited. I was hopeless, and I thought all I could expect in life was pain. *Maybe that's what I deserve?* My parents' unhappiness was my fault. Their arguing was my fault. My family was evidence that forever isn't possible. Love doesn't last and you'll eventually hate each other. I struggled with my mental health and thought I was beyond help. I became a perfectionist finding my worth in work done well. I was anxious, and I often thought of hurting myself. In time, I developed an addiction to escape and cope. Healing came in stages, and while much of it has been completed, there's still work to be done.

I detail most of my mental health journey in my book *Winning the Silent Battle*. Because of that, I am only going to talk about one aspect of it here: self-injury ideation. I know—it's not pretty and somewhat extreme.

Opening up to people wasn't always a good experience. I was always told that I was too sensitive and to get over it. "Learn to take a joke" is something I heard when I was visibly upset by a comment. After a while, I stopped opening up to people; they were untrustworthy. I painted a smile on my face to hide the hurt.

But pain decided it didn't want to be stuffed down in a bottle anymore. It exploded and when it did, the fire felt intense. I felt aches and burns in my heart so much so that it overwhelmed me. I needed relief! I needed an outlet for it. That is when I wanted to turn to cutting. Self-injury is about trying to find a relief for pain, and that is what I thought the razor could bring me. I thought it could save me from the torment. For months I thought about cutting, and each time I did, I could feel the Holy Spirit say, *"Trust Me! I am bringing you through a healing journey."* I wanted to trust Him. I wanted to believe I would be all right and that I could feel real joy. But it was difficult; it was difficult because I didn't know how much God loved me. My head may have known it, but my heart didn't. *God loves me? Me, who is to blame for my parents' marriage? Me, whose voice is annoying? Me, who was often told by my dad that he loves me but I'm weird? Me? Are we talking about the same person?* That's when God took me on a journey of uncovering His love.

It started with love letters. One day at Barnes and Noble, a pink book jumped out at me. It was decked in roses with a title splashed across the front: *His Princess Bride, Love Letters From Your Prince.* Authored by Sheri Rose Shepherd, this book held letters written from Jesus to His bride. Each letter came with a response, and I treated it like a devotional. I read it along with whatever chapter I was reading in the Bible that day. There were letters of love, hope, and healing. Each one helped me see how God's love for me was far deeper than what I'd experienced and greater than I imagined. I was slowly starting to see how my Jesus really felt about me.

One particular day, the pain was really bad. Even though I was starting to get a grasp on God's vast love for me, the temptation to cut myself was still there. On this day, I felt ripped raw, emotionally, like I was drowning in my unbottled pain. I thought about a razor again. It was so easy to get. And if that didn't work, surely a pair of scissors in my room could do the trick. I couldn't take it, and as I started walking toward the razor, I began to have a vision. I was standing with Jesus, and He was asking me not to harm myself. As He asked, He threw Himself between my wrist and the blade I had in my hand. He couldn't let me go through with it. I was stunned. I put the razor down, and every time after that moment when I was tempted to cut, I replayed that vision. I didn't know a lot, but I knew God didn't want me to hurt myself because of His great love

> **In the vision, Jesus was asking me not to harm myself.**

for me. Wow!

I was fortunate to have an amazing mentor when I was in college. I confided in her the pain that I felt and the multiple divorces I had been through as a child. She led me through a study of Song of Solomon. It was her favorite book of the Bible because it's an allegory for Christ's love for the church. We went through a line-by-line study written by Mike Bickel. It was beautiful! Through it, I learned to see myself as not only loved but desired and pursued by God! I started to see myself as part of the Bride that Christ fought for and adored. My favorite verse was 2:14: "Oh my Dove, in the clefts of the rock, in the hiding place on the mountainside let me see your face. Let me hear your voice for your voice is sweet, and your face is lovely." He loved my voice and called me lovely. No "buts" or "even though's." Plain and simple and powerful love.

> **I thought I deserved pain and misery. His love taught me differently.**

My mentor and I started our study my sophomore year of college. I had come a long way, but it wasn't until spring of that year when the fullness of revelation hit: *God loves me.* In my heart, there was a question about relationships that I'd never asked out loud. It only existed in my memory. One night, I went to our InterVarsity Christian Fellowship Large Group meeting where the speaker was talking about evangelism...I think. To be honest, I don't remember his talk—I only remember the five-minute tangent he went on talking about relationships. In that tangent, he answered my question. I couldn't believe it! I had almost forgotten that I even wanted to ask it months prior. That's when the revelation of God's love for me came—so personal and vast. I wanted to run through the halls shouting that Jesus loved me! *He loves me!*

It was important for me to gain revelation of God's love for me, because when I did, I was able to see, trust, and believe that He wants good things for me. I thought I deserved pain and misery. His love taught me differently. What groom wants only misery for his bride? This was an important truth I needed to learn. A few years passed and I continued to pour myself into learning of God's love for me. I also continued putting in the work to reverse the negative impact of trauma and to be a healthy person through mentorship and online therapy videos—a continual journey, and not an easy feat. Just as I had become used to being healthy, my family's disfunction came back for another round.

I started getting calls from my dad asking me why I wasn't there for my brother. He needed a role model and someone to get him back on track. He had done all he could; now it was my turn. But my brother froze me out with everyone else. I prayed for him, and I had seen the fruit of some of those prayers, but I didn't take responsibility for my brother. I had wrongly taken responsibility for my dad and second stepmom's marriage. That was enough.

Fast forward several months to Christmas Eve. I was in my midtwenties. My dad told me that he and his wife were done, and he was bringing his new girlfriend to dinner to meet the rest of the family. He didn't want her to be alone for the holiday and wanted me to make her feel welcome. That was the straw that broke the camel's back. It bothered me that my dad had blamed *me* in the past for unhappiness in his marriage, but I didn't say anything. It wasn't right for him to try to make me responsible for my younger brother's actions, but again I stuffed it down. Now with this on top of it…

It didn't stop at Christmas Eve. Any chance my dad got he would change our plans to include his girlfriend. When I asked if we could hang out just the two of us as initially planned, he rejected it saying they were a package deal. He wasn't listening or allowing me space to come to terms with everything.

That is when I had to step away. It wasn't because I didn't love him nor was it because I didn't like her. I didn't know her. I stepped away because I needed space to grieve another broken marriage. I stepped away to get out from under burdens that weren't mine to carry. I stepped away because I was in too much pain and needed to heal. This family that I loved and wanted to see restored would not be restored. This dream, this hope, would not be reality. My attempts to explain to my dad why I was stepping back from our relationship were ineffective. He didn't listen. He called me judgmental. I couldn't heal around someone who didn't respect or acknowledge that I was in pain.

My dad felt hurt by my decision and lashed out, telling everyone in the family how I was a terrible daughter. I know because I overheard him, and there was an awkward tension between my aunts and uncles and me for a couple years. Whenever we had family get togethers I was not informed or invited. I learned about them after the fact. At Christmas and Thanksgiving, out of nine aunts and uncles, only one aunt would initiate conversation with me and ask me how I was. When I tried to talk with the others, the room got chilly.

While things are neutral between my extended family and me now, it took some time to get there. In the midst of the family drama, I found myself starting to spiral. I'd fully believed that my dad and second stepmom were going to figure things out and their relationship would be saved. When it wasn't, I honestly thought the same cycle of divorce that wreaked havoc on my parents would follow me, and I would be doomed to repeat the cycle. There are two reasons I had been single all my life: First, I thought it best to get healthy before trying to get in a relationship. Less baggage to bring in, right? Second, I was scared of someone being close enough for my heart to get hurt that bad. My attitude was *if divorce is inevitable, why bother?* I'd been swirling in this mindset for a solid week or two before my friend Stu said four words that set me free forever: "The curses are cursed."

The story that prompted him to pray this is his to tell, but I am grateful he did. Hearing those words of truth brought me out of the hopelessness that had begun to consume me. Proverbs 26:2 says "Like a fluttering sparrow or a darting swallow, an undeserved curse does not come to rest."

"The curses are cursed." They hold no more power over my life. Those words snapped me back to reality. I can't change what happened to my parents, but their marriage was not my fault or responsibility. Yes, divorce ran through my immediate and extended family. It happened, and it was a nightmare. But just because it happened, doesn't mean it has to keep happening. I choose to have hope. I take classes on marriage. I choose and take action to be a healthy person mentally, spiritually, emotionally, and physically. I'm working on being healthy financially. Every day I move toward health. I choose to take God at His word. I choose to say no to fear and let hope win.

> **I choose to have hope!**

Before, I thought the victory would be in my parents' marriage getting restored. But it wasn't. My victory came in healing and making the decision to get and stay healthy. My victory came in taking off a pain identity and declaring and believing that I am a child of Love. Someday I'll have a God-centered, happy, and healthy marriage. This is my victory.

"A thousand may fall at your side, ten thousand at your right hand, but it will not come near you." —Psalm 91:7 (NIV)

## Judi Kruis, coach, artist, author

Judi Kruis is an international buyer and began her creative adventures with several years of missions in Latin America doing business and community development outreach in Haiti and Guatemala. An active artist, author, and gardener, she enjoys the mystery and revelation that unfold as she creates, even when things begin with a plan!

One of her paintings in Grand Rapids' famed ArtPrize competition is part of the storyline in the movie *Chasing The Rain*, released in 2020 on Amazon Prime.

As a certified coach with BS degrees in Business Management and Ministry Leadership, Judi loves to guide and encourage others to rediscover and step into their Kingdom callings. She will be restarting her online "RE:WRITE Your Destiny" challenges in late 2023 with the release of her new book.

Judi lives near the lakeshore in Holland, Michigan.

To sign up for her newsletter or to learn more, visit:

**www.JudiKruis.com**

or follow on Instagram and Facebook @jkruiscreations

## CHAPTER ELEVEN
Judi Kruis

# When Faith Looks Like Failure

You might be like me with so many dreams for life—little and big—yet the fear of failure, long-defined comfort zones, and limiting thoughts create a big banner floating through your mind, saying, "I AM NOT ENOUGH. IT WILL NEVER HAPPEN FOR ME." Those were thoughts that plagued me for years. After daring to try and experiencing more failures, my confidence and faith faltered. Until God showed me His perspective...

As a kid, I thought my big adventures would just be an annual trip to a nearby amusement park or camping at the beach. I never dared to think of Disney, plane trips, or international travel, and I didn't have any understanding of God. We were not a church or daily prayer kind of family. I only went occasionally. When I was about 19, I had an impactful altar call. Something shifted in my heart, but my logical brain was still skeptical. A person from the church stayed in touch with me via phone for a year, sharing ways to study the Bible and talking through my questions. God wasn't just working on my heart; He was working on my mind. Even so, I was still hesitant to give my all to the church or God, but the Bible became my guide more than a certain church's teachings.

It was almost ten years later in Holland, Michigan, when a stray Sunday visit to a new church sparked a deeper hunger to explore and understand what a faith journey with Jesus could mean. Soon after, I moved back to my hometown of Grand Rapids and decided to try a few churches to see if more of those sparks could be found. An invitation came to what was called a "seeker church." Their style made it easier for me to understand the life of Jesus and what it meant to be a believer in a relationship with God.

I continued to explore, question, and discover in the hours outside of Sunday mornings. The Bible really came to life during a weeknight group study of the book *Experiencing God* by Henry Blackaby! Under-standing increased in a rich way, and to my biggest surprise, I found I *was* hearing from God! Others didn't seem to be expecting or experiencing this, but it was so clear to me and I could not ignore it.

Many places don't teach that we can hear from heaven, but as I studied and listened, I realized what Jesus meant when He said, "My sheep hear my voice" (John 10:27).

I dug in. It was as if a dam had burst! My hesitations that my free will and freedom would be lost were thrown to the side, and I knew I wanted to follow God as closely as possible. It was a different kind of freedom, richer than I had considered or imagined! My faith and belief that all things were possible with God began to change those negative banners in my mind.

Group studies, journalling, local outreach, and a desire to do missions became a part of life quickly. *Here I am Lord, send me where You need me!*

As I asked and listened, I heard, "Latin America." So, *yes, sign me up for the Mexico trip!* At the age of 38, I took my first mission trip with a friend, having no idea how this simple act of service would change my life and how I thought about following Jesus.

> **My faith and belief that all things were possible with God began to change the negative banners in my mind.**

So much was going on at the same time. The relationship I was in was heading downhill after I discovered many deceptions, yet my relationship with God was blossoming in heavenly truths. Interestingly, it was my fiancé who introduced me to the church. Who would have guessed?

Around the same time, I lost my job, searched for a new one, and happened to find one in Holland where I lived a few years before. I was feeling peace in the midst of loss and chaos surrounding me. The failures were noted but were no longer central in the banner space in my mind.

My new job came with the requirement of finishing my business degree. I was not excited at first. Finding a place to accept my earlier credits in accounting and computer programming courses was difficult. I selected a Christian college with an accelerated program for a bachelor's in business management with ministry leadership. I could study what was needed *and* what I wanted! *Perfect.*

Do we usually think about God's hand guiding us when things line up so well? Things seemed to line up with this, but I was used to only trying to find Him when life fell apart. I don't know where we get the idea that following Jesus and living the dreams He has given us is easy and everything will go smoothly. It was a deep time of stretching my comfort zones and limiting beliefs. Working full-time, college for two years, and extra theology studies in the midst, I was not sure how Latin America would ever fit in again.

One big dream of mine was owning a home. Prior relationships had me waiting, saving, and expecting things to look different. At 40 and still in college in my hometown, I found a great little house close to my new job. Now back in Holland, the city of those first sparks, I was eager to unpack and settle in.

I wanted to remain intentional about preparing for missions, and a church I volunteered with was planning a trip to Malta. It wasn't Latin America, but it seemed a good place to start. *Application in, a deposit made, and my first passport in the works! Yes!* I was so excited and eager to learn and experience more. After a few planning meetings, in my prayer time, I heard God say not to go. He said the missions would come to me. *What? I'm ready. Why wait?*

In a "normal" life, all this happening at once might seem pretty confusing—some days it was. In this new chapter of my life, getting to know the settings, characters, and how it would all come together took some time. Since my relationship had ended, some parts of life were simplified, but my heart yearned for that place of purpose.

Even though I moved 30 minutes away, my prayer partner and I continued to meet and call regularly which was very impactful. One day while praying at my new house, I was talking about what to do with "the office" (the second bedroom). She said, "I see children in that room." I laughed at her. Older and single again, I was past any desire for having kids.

Then, I confessed to her. While asking God about the room the week before, I also heard there would be children. I laughed at Him too, thinking He meant it for a different owner. When something is repeated though, I do take notice! I remembered Hebrews sharing that Sarah was a great woman of faith even though she had laughed at God about children in her "old age" too! *What will this look like for me?*

Shortly after, my friend from the Mexico trip called to see if an exchange student could stay for a week. I said sure, not knowing in a few weeks she would ask if the student could return to my house for the rest of the school year. God gave me the answer before she even called. But how can an already *full* life take on more? That was the start of missions being brought to me and Parenting 404 when I'd never learned 101.

Several people asked me what a single person was doing housing an exchange student. Believe me, I was wondering too. Let me explain Parenting 404. With this student, I was called into the principal's office multiple times. Some might have been due to cultural misunderstandings, but rules were broken, and the student was permanently suspended and sent back to their home country early. A new student from Colombia came soon after who was a great fit and a lot of fun. We even had a double graduation party as I finished my business degree!

Over the summer, a student from Spain stayed for a month of study, and as the school year approached, a fourth student arrived from Mexico. We were trying to get her into a school when she asked about dance classes. Our local arts council offered those, so we signed her up. I thought, *why not take an art class while she's in dance?* Both art and math were my focuses in high school. *Sign me up, too!* Before dance classes started though, they found a school across the state for her. She moved, but art stayed in my weekly plan and was another life changer.

It's easy to fill our days with family and home responsibilities, jobs, and helping with homework, and I realized I was stuck in a grind. Time for learning, interests, and exploration had been set aside.

However, my growth and dreams were important, especially as I listened to where God needed me. After learning to live without TV during my college studies, I was amazed by the things I now had time for.

More opportunities were opening; there were so many things I wanted to do. God was putting new desires in my heart. I realized I didn't have to wait for the students to be out of the house, for an abundance of savings, or retirement! Taking some little steps to prepare can open the doors to even more. This was how it happened for me.

I found some workshops about missions and serving internationally and locally. More testing the waters. On the night of my last Perspectives class on world missions, I came home to an email from a connection working in Haiti. They shared about another group looking for help teaching business skills to artisans in Haiti. *WOW, a perfect fit AND it was Latin America!? Am I really ready?*

Many questions were asked as I met with the new organization, my local connection, and my boss. Logic said there was no way I could go for six weeks when I only had two weeks of vacation. A leave of absence was recommended, and then I could return to my job. *Let's do it!* So often we have a deep faith in God but only see limitations in ourselves or our circumstances. God was bringing opportunities, showing open doors, and smoothing rough places. My faith was growing in myself and in Him. This was still a *big* leap.

After two weeks with the first established group in Haiti, I got on a 14-passenger plane for a short flight to the southern coast. The plane was open and we could see the pilot and co-pilot. They came on the speaker and announced, "We're going to fly over the runway once before landing to warn the kids and the animals to move out of the way."

At that moment, I had a real crisis of wondering if I should have said yes. Of course, I continued on trusting God's plan, and there are many more stories from serving in Haiti. We helped the new group and artisans establish their business processes and made several trips in the coming years. More of this story is shared in my upcoming book, but for now, I'll just say I never thought living without electricity and plumbing would be easier than the abundance of the U.S. Life was simple and somehow more joyful as we would gaze at the stars or sit in the candlelight to sort corn for planting. And by the way, whole kernels are for sowing and those with holes won't grow but will feed the chickens! Everything has a purpose!

Six weeks later, I returned home and back to my corporate work feeling very out of sorts. Anxiety attacks started happening at the grocery store with all the choices and *where did all those people come from?* I did not feel like I belonged at "home" anymore.

Then, my friend from the Mexico trip invited me to Guatemala. *Latin America, here I come again*—more risks and waters to test. It was a great experience! I loved the country, and the team honored the culture and loved the people while doing medical clinics and community development in remote and unreached areas. I was now asking God, *where do I focus and what language do I practice?* For the next seven years, I did trips to both countries. Listeners were probably confused when I used the right words in the wrong country. Sometimes you just need to apologize, smile, and laugh!

After the first Haiti trip, God told me to start a business with my art. *What art? How does this fit with international missions? Is this why You sent missions to me, to bring me back to my creative roots?* There were often more questions than answers.

I didn't laugh at this request, but if you had seen my paintings, you might have! With a few classes under my belt and maybe three good paintings, I did research. A few books, many websites, and an online international art webinar shared several ways to bring income from a creative life. I started with a couple of suggestions. Investing in a special printer, paper, matting, and packaging was simple enough and helped me to multiply inventory quickly for several years! People around me were excited to hear about what I was doing and to see my creative art, rugs, and writings. It seemed promising until…

Several months before the Haiti opportunity, God shared I would leave my job. Two years or two months, He doesn't always give the details. My savings were used on the house, college, and trips, so my apprehensions about income were real. After years in accounting roles, brokerage firms, and local outreach with budget counseling, I knew how money worked. The prospect of being without my nice income didn't look extremely promising—maybe another reason FAITH is spelled R.I.S.K.

Nine months after returning from the first trip to Haiti, God said it was time to leave. This was in late 2007 and 2008's recession made selling art a bit difficult. I remained involved with international things and started some contract work, consulting, and part-time positions for small businesses and nonprofits. More water testing! The numbers in my budget, however, were not adding up. God was encouraging and reassuring me I was on the right path and that all would work out. We had some intense conversations...or I did anyway. It wasn't my faith in Him wavering as much as doubting myself, as more and more of my focus turned to my circumstances. I was at the end of what I could do financially. The house He told me not to sell, a few years later ended up in foreclosure. Most people around me did not even know. I didn't dare share much since it seemed I was failing God.

How does following God bring something this devastating? *God, if all these trips, this call to Latin America, and creating a business with art were from You, how can it lead to more failure? Where did I go wrong? How can I change this? What are YOU going to do?* The messages on the banner in my mind were getting muddy again.

I realized during much of this journey, I was trying to do things with my own strength, controlling input, outcomes, processes, and more. I was following what God said, *but* I wasn't always taking steps *with* Him. I was being transformed by the renewing of my mind (Romans 12:2), going from a control freak and perfectionist, used to being stubbornly independent and having to do it all on my own, to learning what it meant to be a beloved daughter of a generous King who wanted to give me good and perfect gifts.

One of the best answers to prayer I had in that season was when God shared, "I didn't call you to success, I called you to obedience."

Oh my…

Sometimes our greatest success is just in our obedience when we hear and follow what God is asking us to do. Relying on my measures of success through money, the opinions of others, and my feelings of comfort or understanding did not help. With obedience as the new definition of success, let's look in the rearview mirror at the perceived failures.

> **Sometimes our greatest success is just in our obedience.**

When it came to relationships and Parenting 404, I took on other people's failures as my own. Wrong focus. I am not at fault for others' actions. When I got this house, I created a big canvas with Isaiah 56:7: "My house will be a house of prayer for all nations." Through the years, I have hosted exchange students from four countries, visitors from even more countries, the homeless, struggling, those preparing for missions, and others beginning their new chapters. God knew what "the office" needed to be used for. It was not all easy, but He shared how happy He has been with my hospitality and my home is often called "the house of peace."

Hearing the words *Latin America*, I thought I would move to another country. My time serving abroad allowed me to see and understand the diversity of other cultures and the vulnerabilities both locally and internationally. A big lesson was seeing how helping in the wrong ways hurts so many. The success has been in my personal formation, preparation, and willingness. My current work has me buying products from other countries. Maybe Latin America was only a starting place, not my final destination!

Why spend thousands on a business degree to become a "starving artist?" Those were not my thoughts but what others said over my life. We don't always notice the word curses we say to ourselves or what others plant in our minds. I learned the impact of labels and limiting mindsets as I rediscovered the person God called me to be. I have both a business and creative mind and spirit. I was only living half of a life, and now I would confidently say life is full and abundant with great hope for the future! I know I am worth investing in so I will have more to share with others!

Giving up so much to serve God, I never expected to see a foreclosure notice or such lean years, but I experienced God's provision and encouragement in such beautiful ways. He continues urging me to dream bigger and not settle for mediocrity—not in prideful expectancy but by trusting His promises. Creative solutions helped get the mortgage reset and some very appreciated help along the way has enabled this house of peace and prayer to serve even more!

Rediscovering my creative spirit and experiencing the impact and value of creativity was worth every sacrifice! Our spirit comes alive in creative times, whether through worship, gardening, woodworking, cooking, or in business. The most interesting details overlooked by my logical brain are now seen with new excitement. Logic can block the Holy Spirit when we stay there all the time, so I don't plan to do that anymore! The control/perfectionist tendencies which led to stress and frustration were replaced with banners of peace, wonder, and exploration.

> **Our spirit comes alive in creative times.**

Breakthrough and success do not always look like we imagine. Even Ephesians 3:20 says, "Now to him who is able to do immeasurably more than all we ask or imagine, according to his power that is at work within us." The most important part of our grounding is God's words of Truth in the Bible. Our experiences, God's guidance, and our obedience to work *with* Him enable us to be shaped for what's ahead. Discovering more about myself and what I was created to be didn't come from the easiest areas in my life but from moving past perceived limitations, experiencing inner healing, and reaching out to serve others.

I have lived more fully and fruitfully in my latter years than my former (Haggai 2:9), and I don't see this momentum stopping!

## **Yvonne Mutch**, author, prophetic minister, teacher, speaker

Yvonne Mutch is a certified prophetic minister with Emerging Prophets School of Ministry, and as often as she has opportunity she loves sharing her testimony, gladdening hearts with Good News, and helping believers get fully grounded in truth so they can live more abundantly and triumphantly. Yvonne has authored numerous books and e-books, including *Smack In The Middle of Love: My Journey Toward Health and Wholeness* and *Strategies for Victory: What I Learned from My Favorite Bible Heroes.* In her previous season, Yvonne home-educated her four children while serving in children's ministry and alternative education for 25+ years, tutoring, teaching, advocating, writing, and publishing in publications such as *Homeschooling Today* and *The Upper Room*, and developing curriculum. She also served as a librarian for various churches and the San Diego County Library.

Yvonne has lived all over the U.S. and currently lives in Albany, Oregon, with Bruce, her musician-artist husband—the brave man who proposed to her 35 years ago and sealed the deal six weeks later. She loves adventure, travel, visits to the coast, reading memoirs, worship that involves movement, and reading aloud to the five youngest of her eight grandchildren.

Yvonne would love to hear from you through either her personal Facebook page or via email at rising2faith@gmail.com. Additionally, you can connect with Yvonne through her Instagram community @tothenations1111, Facebook business profile @GodsGrammarGirl (which serves as her alter ego), or her new Facebook community called New Covenant Triumphant.

### Email Yvonne at: **rising2faith@gmail.com**
### Learn more at:

# Silent and Shameful No More

"That's okay, you can just get an abortion, and I'll pay for it," were the words I heard when I found myself pregnant for the first time at age 17. This wasn't the response I was expecting. After all, my older boyfriend was the adult in our relationship, but I fully expected him to say, "Let's get married." In my naivete, I assumed he'd man-up and take responsibility for the baby in my womb. Not only was he unwilling to become a father, he was also unwilling to enter the abortion clinic. He simply dropped me as if it were a common errand, forcing me to deal with the responsibility and the terror alone.

Once inside the clinic's prep room, I was surprised to find a similar story amongst the other frightened young women I encountered—we were all on birth control when we found ourselves pregnant. This wasn't supposed to happen, but this was the aftermath of the sexual revolution. *We were supposed to be "free" and shielded from pregnancy, but alas, here we are, learning our lesson the hard way.* At any rate, I'll always remember the fear and helplessness I felt that day. Everything in me wanted to cry out, "Stop!" but I didn't know how to make it stop. Instead, I forced myself to bear the horror of the situation and endure what the clinic counselors told me was my best option. They also counseled me that there was no need to inform my parents, and thus, I kept my silence.

Feeling utterly sick afterward, I held myself together until I climbed into my boyfriend's truck. As we drove away, I let loose with what can only be described as *wailing*. I was in physical pain, yes, but deep within, I knew this truth: two lives had entered the clinic that day, but only one life walked out. Even sadder was the fact that I didn't yet know this man was an alcoholic, he didn't love me, and worse yet, he was a predator. When he took advantage of me a few

119

months later, I became pregnant again, and this time, he wasn't so polite. "I don't have the money to pay for another abortion. You'll have to go down to the welfare office and let the government pay for it."

To this day, the most humiliating moment of my life was sitting in that welfare office, alone, facing a man who exuded the harshest judgment toward me. Today, it seems it would have been a more equitable situation if my boyfriend had been required to sit beside me and face what was also his responsibility. The only upside to this humiliation was that I had a wake-up call to who this man was and broke it off with him. However, a vicious cycle of relationships with men had already begun, and I allowed myself, time and again, to be demeaned and de-valued because I didn't value myself.

I share this abortion thread of my story only to share the larger thread. Growing up without knowing God, and without the knowledge of how precious and worthy I was in His eyes, I had no comprehension of my worth. No one ever told me this truth. No one ever spoke about how valuable Yvonne was. I didn't recognize my own value and treated myself accordingly. Even after I met Jesus I struggled through the process of seeing myself how God sees me. My vision remained clouded.

**No one ever spoke of how valuable Yvonne was.**

Sadly, my life wasn't going as planned. Prior to my first pregnancy, I can still picture sitting in my bedroom one afternoon with my best girlfriend, envisioning the future we'd mapped out for ourselves. I remember saying, "I'll have one child and see how it goes, and if I like it, I'll have two." At nearly 16 years of age there was no way I could know my life was about to spiral out of control, and I would live through a multitude of misadventures including (but not limited to) heavy drug use, promiscuity, and running away from home and ending up on the streets of both New York City and Miami-Dade County Florida. In part, this was because I got caught up in the aftermath of the sexual revolution and the lies that were propagated at the time. Believing a number of lies, I thought I was free to give myself away, that somehow this empowered me. This lie combined with my lack of self-worth—or perhaps it enhanced my lack of self-worth—caused me to lose sight of the right I had to protect myself and my body. The thought of saying *no* to whatever men wanted from me somehow escaped my understanding.

At any rate, after surviving the enormously stupid decision to run away from home—which included a Greyhound bus ride to New York and hitch-hiking from New York to Miami—I found my way back home to San Diego, re-entered high school, and miraculously graduated with my class. Although I returned to a life with a parental roof over my head, I found myself living with a new normal severely lacking in boundaries. Minus the pot-smoking, I was free to do whatever I wanted, and that's what led me into the arms of the man I've mentioned; the man who didn't value me and set the tone for the way I would allow myself to be treated by men. I had no business being in a relationship with him in the first place, but no one advised me otherwise or protected me from him. The man was an alcoholic and a predator who raped me in the middle of the night, causing the very pregnancy he disdained. Thankfully, my story doesn't end here.

My next relationship was far more equitable, and although we were young and unprepared when we found ourselves pregnant, we were willing to do the right thing and get married. Facing my mom, however, was no easy task. She was now a college student and headstrong feminist. All she'd been denied in life was what she now wanted for me: college, career, control. She didn't want me repeating her life: married at 19, giving birth to her first child one month before turning 20, and working a job she hated for 20 years. So, when we all sat around the family table that fateful afternoon, my mom and step-dad laid out, with great insistence, all the reasons my boyfriend and I shouldn't get married or have this baby. My mom became a formidable opponent. In the end, despite my boyfriend's desire to keep the baby, I succumbed and endured another hellish experience, continuing to maintain my secrets. I believe I would have kept this baby if I'd had anything resembling a support system, but my boyfriend's family was imploding. He was losing the roof over his own head. I believe he just didn't have the emotional strength to fight the decision or to give me the support I needed.

For three more years I carried the growing weight of my shame.

> **I carried the growing weight of my shame.**

Exploring my way through college, I attempted to fulfill my mother's dreams of me becoming an independent woman. However, as I tried out one major after another, I was slipping into a dark place and losing my grip on my sanity, hope, and purpose. I remember well the day I came to the edge of a dark chasm, and, although I knew it would be easier to allow myself to fall into it, I chose not to. Perhaps what kept me going and what ultimately saved me was my quest for truth. *Surely I will find the truth.* Indeed it was a winding road of exploring an array of New Age beliefs and other practices born of the dark side before someone introduced me to the love of Jesus. I tell more of the story in my memoir called *Smack In the Middle of Love,* but in essence, I was the woman at the well who had a "Road to Damascus" experience, hearing the audible voice of the Lord saying, "I'm cleansing you of your sins."

And thus, I began my tumultuous journey with the Lord as a 21-year-old, single mother of a six-month-old baby girl, on welfare, getting high daily, and already separated from the father of my child after a string of unhealthy relationships with men and the consequences that go with it. You might think that because I heard the audible voice of the Lord the stars would align in my favor and vanquish all my enemies. I certainly did hear Him. However, I encountered the well-worn truth *wherever I go, there I am.* Alongside the battle of encountering demonic assault because of my involvement with certain occult practices, I faced the battle of getting free of my stinking grave clothes. Yes, I was graced with a new heart, but the transformation of my mind, will, and emotions was another thing entirely. Deleting old mindsets and getting free of their attached behaviors was no easy task. Hiding my pregnancy for 20 weeks in order to bring to birth my first baby was the beginning of my turn-around. But my old mindsets would continue to prevail for a number of years. Isn't it interesting how seemingly innocuous comments made to us as children make such strong imprints upon our developing psyches and spirits?

So here I was now, in the midst of motherhood, going it alone as best as I could, living the life neither my mother nor myself had envisioned. My children's father—Dave, who's been residing in heaven a long while now—wasn't able to help much either physically or financially, as he was a hemophiliac, made frequent visits to the hospital, and lived on disability payments from the government. Additionally, he took a lot of prescription medication for the pain he lived with, not to mention the alcohol and other recreational drugs thrown in for good measure. In fact, it was Dave who'd introduced me to smoking pot as a lifestyle, which quickly became my coping mechanism to avoid facing myself and my situation head on. But, I must give credit to this man for encouraging me to choose life and to not have another abortion. Because by this time, I was well-acquainted with the emotional pain and trauma of abortion as well as the potential physical complications abortions can cause. In fact, I'd already panicked and aborted our first baby during one of Dave's long absences (my fourth abortion). I'm reminded even now of a quote I once heard somewhere: "Abortion as a solution is as effective as an animal chewing off its leg to get out of the trap it's in." Abortion truly is the worst of solutions.

Believing abortion was a solution, albeit an imperfect one, was only one of the many lies I believed. The chief lie I believed was that I wasn't good or worthy enough to begin serving God just as I was, as a single, unmarried mother. Adding to my lack of value for myself, I believed the falsehood that I had to be "better" or fixed up a bit to begin my walk with the Lord.

I remember my one overriding thought at the time: *surely God would want me to be married,* and believing this distorted version of truth, I took action to help God out with this matter. Because I refused to allow God to write a new script for my life (and because I initiated one disastrous decision after another), I entered into the volatile and tumultuous years I now refer to as the "broken chapter" of my life.

These years almost cost me the life of one of my daughters, her father, and myself.

All of this could have been avoided, however, had I understood the truth of who I was and the truth of who God is—an accepting and loving Heavenly Father whose love has no strings or conditions attached. That was another lie I believed—that love always has conditions, and I had to give myself to men for them to love me. All the while, I didn't understand it was the love of my Heavenly Father I needed to receive rather than seeking the imperfect love of imperfect men.

And so it was, armed with the misbelief that *surely God would want me to be married*, I plunged into a relationship with a man I barely knew. Although I'd once had an eight-day fling with this man, I had no way of knowing when I encountered him two years later that he was fresh out of prison on charges of attempted manslaughter, and

> **It was the love of my Heavenly Father I needed to receive rather than seeking the imperfect love of imperfect men.**

even his own family feared him. He was nothing less than a wolf in sheep's clothing. In less than one week's time, we went down to Tijuana and said our vows before a justice of the peace.

The marital bliss lasted all of five days before he punched me in the face. When I sought a marriage annulment, I was denied because my marriage certificate hadn't been properly notarized at the courthouse. Therefore, I wasn't legally married. This would have been good news, except for when I sought spiritual counsel, two different ministers told me I *was* married in the eyes of God because of the marriage vows I'd recited. Additionally, this abusive man, with "marriage" certificate in hand, didn't want to let me go. Although he moved out, he kept close watch on all my actions. My life, at this point in time, began to resemble a badly-written soap opera. Sadly, however, I wasn't yet ready to hand the reins of my life over to God.

Still writing my own script, and with the new storyline being *surely God would want me to reconcile with my child's father*, I hatched a plan to escape Mr. Convicted Felon's constant threats. In short order, I turned down an offer for Section 8 housing, sold what little I had, and drove across the country, only to find my child's father wasn't ready for marriage. The fact that he wasn't ready for a more permanent commitment came to light in this way: One day, in our newly-secured apartment, he picked up what little money was left and asked if I wanted anything from the store. "Orange juice," was my response, not knowing I wouldn't see him for another three weeks. He left me with no food, our one-year-old daughter (he missed her birthday), and a brand-new baby in my womb. The local food bank workers took pity on me and gave me minimal food rations once a week instead of once a month. One week, my diet consisted of government cheese and powdered refried beans. Things such as this are not easily forgotten. But the upside of this tough situation is that I began my journey of becoming an overcomer. I didn't yet know it, but I was learning that God is my Provider, Protector, and Defender.

Four months later, I found my way back home to an old bedroom in my mom's house. Unbeknownst to me, my mom had arranged a drive to Los Angeles for a mid-term abortion, but to escape this fate, I declared I'd give my baby up for adoption. For the next five months I did the best I could to convince myself I could do this hard thing and began working with an adoption agency. My low self-worth continued, and becoming a welfare recipient again didn't help. At the same time, Mr. Felon was in prison again for multiple violations of his parole, one of them being methamphetamine use. This gave me a false sense of security, and I made the mistake of opening up communications with him, and this thorn in my flesh would continue to prick even deeper during this most broken chapter of my life. I was lonely, but yet I didn't turn to the One who is the true lover of my soul.

**Some decisions I made were the result of operating with a heart full of wounds.**

Around this same timeframe, I made another horrendous decision. Allowing my pride to get the better of me, I stopped going to church when it was the fellowship of the saints I needed the most. Some decisions I made seem incomprehensible now, and perhaps they were the result of operating with a heart full of wounds. At any rate, I was emotionally ill-equipped to deal with what I encountered each time I walked through a new set of church doors with my baby in tow and my growing tummy. Instead of being welcomed with, "Hello! Good Morning!" I was greeted by religious church gate-keepers asking, "Is your husband at home?" Thankfully, I would later encounter a church that supported and nurtured me in my messy condition.

*Smack in the Middle of Love* is aptly named—a reminder to me that He was always with me, even in the midst of my unloveliness. And even after I came to know Him, He patiently waited for me to fully surrender my life to Him. He was and is that good. But to ensure you understand the full measure of God's redemption of my life, and the extent of His mercy and goodness toward me in the midst of all of my failures and mistakes, allow me to share a few more snapshots of this disastrous season only God could mend.

During this time, I gave birth to my second daughter and kept her, bought an old one-bedroom trailer and moved it up into the mountains, continued communications with the ex-felon (which led to visiting him while in prison), and fell into a lifestyle of getting high again. Over the next two years, I lived dangerously, tangled between relationships with my children's father and the convicted felon which ultimately ended in a near-death experience for my children's father. Yes, it was a modern-day showdown between two men. One had a gun, but the other had a car and ran over the one with a gun. I was already living in the hospital with my oldest daughter who had a life-threatening illness when I got the call: "Yvonne, sit down. I have some bad news. Dave's been hit by a car and he's in surgery right now to relieve the pressure on his brain, but he's not expected to make it." Compounded with this news was the discovery that Dave had HIV and both myself and my two daughters had been exposed.

This was my wake-up call, and my journey back to God began. Unbelievable perhaps, but it took nothing less than my daughter and her father's miraculous healing for my eyes to be opened to the truth that I couldn't continue to live the life I was living.

I would later discover God's preservation of my own life. It came to light that a man who came to my home three times "looking for Dave's girl-friend," was connected to the mafia and was looking to settle a score with the man (Dave) who owed him money for a gun. I'd chatted pleasantly with this man the first time he'd arrived at my doorstep, but after Dave woke up from his coma, I learned what horrific things were occurring on the other side of his conversation with me. In essence, this man was coming back to my door with retribution on his mind, and he'd already made it clear to Dave what he was capable of and willing to do.

This is but one instance of how God used what the enemy meant for evil for His good and how He preserved my life, time and again. He patiently waited for me because He had a plan for my life. The enemy would rather have silenced me, but God has called me to proclaim the Good News. Many of my lessons were learned the hardest way possible, but everything I went through had its purpose and brought me to where I am today. I love nothing more than to testify of what I'm intimately acquainted with: God's goodness, love, and forgiveness toward all who would receive it, no matter their past. We can trust Him, even with our lives. I've also had the opportunity to testify in the Oregon State Senate to help pass legislation to eliminate abortions performed without parental consent and to testify why life-saving medical equipment should be required in every abortion facility.

> **No one is beyond the reach of God's love and redemption, and no situation is too hard for Him to restore and redeem.**

Testifying in such a manner, however, was only the beginning of me being *silent no more*. I owe Him my very life and cannot help but to proclaim what my life vividly portrays: that no one is beyond the reach of the power of God's love and redemption, and no situation is too hard for Him to restore and redeem. The enemy tried to destroy me, but I'm still standing.

The earthly father in Luke 11 beautifully portrays the extravagant love of our Heavenly Father who receives back his prodigal sons and daughters with arms wide open. Even beyond this, the earthly father bestowing the best robe, a new ring, and sandals upon his son signifies the high value we have in our Heavenly Father's eyes. Indeed, His value for us exceeds what we deserve and what we can imagine. As for me, I had to face death and break free of the lies I believed about myself in order to find my way back to the Father and come into agreement with my true identity—a beloved daughter of a Most High God, highly cherished and highly valued. This was the beginning of my journey toward health and wholeness and walking in truth. And as I continue to walk with Him, each step becomes sweeter and sweeter. Restoration is a beautiful thing.

"For He who is mighty has done great things for me, and holy is His name." —Luke 1:49 (Mary's song)

## Heather Ferrante, pastor, author, entrepreneur

Heather is a passionate Kingdom Lifestyle and Beauty Influencer who is on a mission to make a difference and see transformation in everything she puts her hands to. This is evident in her role as a professional hairstylist and makeup artist, in addition to her many projects through the years as a traveling minister, singer, and songwriter.

She is the founder of Esther's Arise – a Facebook community for women to connect with other amazing women around the world who love Jesus, want to grow deeper in their God given identity, and be able to walk in and release their beauty, creativity, and favor as modern day Esthers.

She is the author of *Free to Dream* and a children's book called *The Happy Place* which are both available on Amazon. She is also a Creative Consultant who has served more than 25 years as an industry expert and community development manager for non-profits, schools, and businesses.

She loves to speak life and hope into people and help them get breakthrough, so that they can step into their dreams.

Her greatest joy is spending time in God's presence or with her family. Making people, places and spaces look beautiful, traveling the world, and championing others to live and love on purpose.

In her free time you'll find her spending time at the beach, hosting friends and events, or doing something creative.

Join Heather Ferrante's Facebook community now at:

**www.facebook.com/groups/truthliesandlattes**

# The Revival Fire

I'll never forget when I was attending Bible college back in the late 90's. A few friends and I were hanging out in our dorm's common area when some girl walked in and started sharing about a fresh outpouring of the Holy Spirit happening at a church in Florida— Brownsville Assembly of God. There were reports of people waiting in line for hours just to be able to get into the main auditorium where church services were held. She then shared with us a video tape of one of the meetings where a young girl was sharing her personal testimony of experiencing God. As we watched this video, the presence of God got so thick and tangible in the room, stirring a deep hunger in our hearts. Instantly we knew we needed to find a way to get there and experience this move of God firsthand as soon as possible.

I had about $65 in my bank account and a full tank of gas at the time. *Hmm, that won't get us very far,* but faith rose up inside of my heart and I volunteered to drive. I felt like God would meet our level of hunger if we decided to go. And that is where this story begins. Little did we know how much our lives would be changed by leaning into the gentle nudge of the Holy Spirit. A day or so later, three friends from college hopped in my little black Dodge Daytona, and the four of us set off on a 14-hour drive across the country with very little cash and no place to stay.

One thing we did have after watching that video was great hope and expectation to encounter God in a fresh way. We were desperate. Our young lives up until that point were met with some challenging circumstances and family dynamics. We not only wanted God to show up in our lives and our families' lives, but we each needed a divine intervention and freedom at a whole different level. We wanted more for our futures and were willing to do whatever it took to meet with

God. We set off on an adventure that would forever change our lives.

We drove all night and all day, and 14 hours later we arrived in Pensacola, Florida. We even made a stop at my

**We were willing to do whatever it took to meet with God.**

family's favorite beach vacation spot in Destin, Florida. It was amazing. When we arrived in town, we noticed a sign for Motel 6. The price on the sign outside was in our budget—having less than $150 between the four of us girls—so that's where we decided to stay. I remember walking into the motel lobby excited to get a room and get settled after driving for so many hours. But much to our dismay, the woman at the desk said there was no room in the inn. So many people were coming to town to be a part of the revival that the rooms were completely booked. We were shocked. We knew we didn't have enough money to stay anywhere else, so we *had* to stay there. Something had to open up for us.

So, back to the car we went, and the first thing we did was pray. "God, we believe You called us to come here for the weekend and believe You have something very special for us here in Florida, so we ask right now, in Jesus' name, that a room would open up for us." In faith we walked back into that lobby and asked her again. "Are you sure you don't have any rooms available for the next two nights? Just one? Can you please look again?"

She looked at us in disbelief but checked her computer. She said, "I'm not sure how this happened, but I have one room that just became available. It's yours if you'd like it." *YES! We knew it!* We were so excited and booked our room. Miracle number one was right there in front of us, and it immediately built up our faith. We went back to the car, grabbed the other girls and our overnight bags, and got settled into our room.

After getting cleaned up, we headed off to attend the nightly meeting. When we pulled into the church parking lot, the line to get into the main auditorium was wrapped around the building several times. Apparently, the lines were growing by the hundreds daily. People were traveling from all over the world to see what God was doing in this special place. When we saw the line, we got a little discouraged because we didn't think we'd be able to get in. Yet God had a special plan for us, and another miracle was about to unfold.

We showed up several hours early on that Friday night to stand in line. A few of us girls needed to use the restroom, but the buildings weren't open. My friend looked at the back of the property and noticed a little house back there. She said, "Hey, maybe they'll let us use their restroom." Her faith was great, mine was not, so I opted to stay in line to hold our place while they went to see if that was a possibility. They came back with four little pieces of pink paper and a story. Not only did this little old man let them use the restroom, but he was one of the elders of the church and a caretaker of the property. The girls shared our story about driving down, and he gave us special passes to get us into the main auditorium for the revival services for the entire weekend—this included Sunday morning, which was reserved just for local church members and their friends with passes. *Wow, God, miracle number two!* That was amazing.

We were one of the last few who were able to get into the main building for service that night. I remember sitting in the very back of the balcony watching Lindell Cooley (the worship leader) and the choir singing our favorite worship songs and praising God with such joy and holy reverence. It was beautiful. We even saw the girl who shared her testimony on the video we saw at the dorm. The place was packed, the overflow was packed, and people were literally running to the altars, getting saved, healed, and delivered. It was incredible to see and experience.

That night, God stirred a holy hunger in our hearts in such a special way. We could have left after that and received so much, but God still had more in store. Saturday night we returned with even greater expectation. My friend was hesitant to go in because the presence of God was different from anything we had ever known. We made it onto the main level that night. Up until that point I had never experienced the presence of God that strong. People all around us were falling out, shaking, getting healed, being delivered from demonic oppression, and being set free. One of my best friends started shaking so violently that the ushers came and took her out of the main room and into a back room where many more people were experiencing the same thing. I'm not going to lie...I was pretty freaked out. We were all freaked out. *What is happening?* But my sense was that God was doing a special deep healing in her life, and I wasn't going to let them take her without the rest of us. Off to the back room we all went.

They led us into a back room full of other people encountering God in the same way. People were crying, laughing, shaking, and laying on the floor undone by the weighty glory of God. There was such a holy reverence in that place. The awesomeness and majesty of God was very real and tangible. People were receiving healing at a very deep level, including us. I'll never forget that night. After receiving prayer, the ushers led us back into the main auditorium right through the doors next to the stage where Steve Hill and John Kilpatrick (the leaders of the revival) were ministering.

Next thing you know, they laid hands on our heads and ministered to us. We were completely undone. God met us that night and we've never been the same. When it was time to head back to the hotel, we were so overwhelmed by God's presence that we were either crawling back to my car or being carried out. This encounter lasted into the night. I remember thinking *I could go back to college now; I've already received so much.* But we still had one more day in Florida before making the long drive back to Missouri.

Sunday morning came and we used our little pink guest slips to get into the main auditorium. It was great. During the offering, my friend Mary leaned over to me and said, "Hey, I have this money I've saved for something special, and I feel like God is saying to write a check for the whole thing and give it." I think it was around $250. I said, "Well, if you really believe God wants you to give it, then you'd better do it." My faith was still growing at that point, but I knew obedience was a big deal to God. With her hand trembling, she, in great faith, wrote the

> **My faith was still growing, but I knew obedience is a big deal to God.**

134

check. It was all the money she had to her name. At that point our group finances were also all depleted, and we still needed to eat and pay for gas for our 14-hour drive back to Bible college. But God wasn't done with our story in Florida.

Immediately after service, the little old man who let the girls use the restroom at his house came up and said he'd be honored if we let him take us out to lunch before our journey home. We were hungry and knew that was another answer to prayer. After lunch, he handed us an envelope with enough cash to get us back home. We were so grateful and excited that God had come through for us yet again! He was meeting us along the way and growing our faith in Him.

Just as we were pulling away in the car, the kind old man waved us down to get our attention and then handed Mary a check. She didn't look at it until we drove away, but it was a check for $500— double what Mary felt like she was supposed to give in the offering that day.

Time after time God showed up so powerfully during the trip for us girls. He was teaching us that He knows us at a very deep level and how He wanted the absolute best for us as we continued to journey through life with Him at the center.

That trip marked my life—it was one of the many memorial stones throughout my journey. Just a few months later, God opened the door for me to start the life adventure with my soon-to-be husband. Keith and I were married a year later and moved to California to be youth pastors at a church he'd grown up in during his high school years. Five months into youth ministry, our senior leader decided to leave, and we were presented with the opportunity to lead the church. So, at the young age of 23, we found ourselves as the senior pastors of this little church in Willits, California.

Keith was so in love with Jesus and very zealous for the Lord, but had some religious mindsets that were a bit challenging at times. He was very skeptical of my encounters with God and my time in Brownsville. Little did I know that the encounter I had in Florida with my girlfriends was getting ready to happen again in a different and fresh way. This time it would be one to forever change the legacy of our family.

This was what I was praying for. I wanted my life to be different than it was growing up. I wanted my

> **I wanted my life and family to be different than it was growing up.**

entire family to experience the fullness of God and His love. I wanted my kids to grow up with parents who truly loved Jesus and put Him first in their lives. I wanted them to experience as much of Jesus as we could here on this earth, this side of Heaven—especially since this wasn't the case for me.

You see, I grew up walking on eggshells in my home. My mom raised me and my three siblings in church, but my dad was never on board with the whole *God thing* and would rarely step foot in a church building. He'd tell me, "Oh, Heather, God might be real, but He's good for *you*. I'm good without Him. I don't need any of that church stuff." Those words would break my heart when I'd hear them, knowing that was the furthest thing from the truth. It was a flat out lie. Unfortunately, my dad fought the truth his whole life here on this earth, right up until the very end, where, by God's grace, I got to pray with him and he accepted Jesus. He lived warring against the truth of God's Word, and his actions were not always loving or kind.

However, that's not God's intention for any of us. John 10:10 says, "A thief comes to steal, kill and destroy, but I have come that you have life, life abundantly." God's desire for us is to walk in His fullness, in His abundant life. With God, there is *hope*! Have you ever looked up the definition of the word *hope*? The word hope means the *joy filled expectation of good things coming your way*. In Christ we have hope! But through the journey with my dad, God taught me how to love and hang onto hope in the midst of it all. I wanted more for my dad while he was alive and will continue to contend for my whole family and the generations to come.

Have you ever believed lies from the enemy? Maybe you grew up in a situation like me where your family dynamics weren't exactly the Cleaver's. God wants us to partner with Him to break the lies the enemy has been speaking to you and your family.

God had to show up for me early on so I could go into marriage with a greater level of faith for what was to come. He changed the course of my generations one summer at a family camp up in the beautiful California redwoods. Keith was on the camp board, and he and I were leading worship together for our summer family camp. Bill Johnson and David Crone were the camp speakers. Both men of God had been experiencing similar life-changing outpourings of the Holy Spirit in their churches, just as I had experienced in Brownsville. When my husband heard they were coming, he got on the phone with Bill and had a conversation. Keith was very skeptical but moved forward with having them at the camp. Little did he know our lives were about to be radically changed for the better.

God's presence started moving at the camp, and I watched my husband transform before my eyes. I remember sitting at this little café after one of the morning services, and I started feeling the Holy Spirit. I started giggling, and Keith thought I was laughing at him. The giggles got louder and I couldn't stop laughing. He got mad. We left the restaurant and went back to the camp, and I knew God was about to do something big. I had forgotten my Bible in the chapel, so we walked over to get it. At that moment, David and Deborah Crone and Mark and Tammy Hawkins were walking out of the chapel. They looked at each other and said, "It's time," then greeted us.

They said, "Hey, guys! Great to see you. Would it be okay if we spent some time and prayed with you?" We agreed, and for the next two hours, they prayed and prophesied over us, speaking into all different areas of our lives. We had never experienced anything like that before. God showed them things we'd never shared with anyone. I remember Keith saying, "Wow, I feel like I've literally just seen Jesus in their eyes." That encounter changed him and us. Those couples let the love of God flow through them in a way that also forever marked us.

From that point on, we started seeking God in a fresh way. Both of us now had experienced and tasted more of God and we wanted it. We wanted it for ourselves, for our church, for our families, and the children we would soon have. We were hungry, and we did whatever we could to be in the presence of God. We started traveling to meetings where God was moving. We'd stay there for hours. God started doing something in us and in our church family.

I remember one day we were up at Bethel Church in Redding for a leader's conference. We'd just had our first child. Bill Johnson was speaking and said something to all of us about young leaders and students in their School of Ministry wanting to have coffee with him. When people asked this, he would say, "I'm happy to have coffee with you. Come back in 20 years and tell me you're still serving and pursuing the presence of God in your life, and then we'll have coffee together."

Over 20 years have now passed from that initial meeting with Bill. This was when my husband and I told God we never wanted our family to be on the backside of a move of God ever again, especially after experiencing His presence in such a tangible way. That has been our prayer ever since. And now, once again, God is pouring His Spirit out in a fresh way. In America, we're seeing it break out on the beaches and college campuses. People are compelled by the love of God to gather once again, and God is reviving His bride all over the earth. It's so incredible watching the generations pursuing God's presence with no specific agenda other than to minister and love on Him.

> **We never wanted our family to be on the backside of a move of God ever again.**

A few weeks ago, I was sitting in my living room having quiet time. The following morning, I planned to hop on a plane to visit my son who was attending Bethel School of Supernatural Ministry (BSSM). As I sat there, I sensed the Holy Spirit say to *turn on Bethel TV*. So, I did. Immediately after worship ended, one of the church leaders walked onto the stage with three BSSM students. She announced, "These students are going to prophesy over some of the visitors tonight." I didn't see who the students were at first, but when the camera zoomed in, there he was—my handsome son Micah—front and center. He was up on stage with a smile on his face, searching the room, looking for the people God wanted to highlight.

He was one of the three chosen to publicly give a word in a packed-out service at Bethel in revival culture. I sat there with joyful tears streaming down my face—this was a full-circle moment with God.

For years we've been praying and contending for revival, for God's presence to manifest here on this earth, and we're seeing measures of it all over the world. And now we're seeing our own young-adult children cry out and contend for the same. I say all of this to encourage you. There is more for you. There is more for your family. Keep pressing in and believing for your God-given inheritance. If you're hungry for more, find a place where God is pouring out His Spirit and go.

> **Keep pressing in and believing for your God-given inheritance!**

If you're finished with the chapter of life you are on and desire something fresh and new, turn the page and ask God to show you how He wants to partner with you in *this* season. A new chapter with God might just change the course of your life and your family's life like it did for me.

## Rosanne Roberts Archuletta, author, dream coach

Rosanne Roberts Archuletta was raised near the Pocono Mountains of Pennsylvania in a small town called Bangor. She spent much of her adult life living and creating a business in San Francisco. For nearly a decade, Rosanne was an Instructor and Business Coach at the Renaissance Entrepreneurship Center. Moving to New Mexico in 2003, she continued growing her business. Continuing her interest in supporting small business, she has been on the Statewide Advisory Board of the New Mexico Small Business Development Center since 2008.

Since 1989, Rosanne has been the Principal of R.M. Roberts and Associates, a human resources consulting firm that provides training, coaching, and staff recruiting to organizations throughout the U.S. She is a dynamic speaker who has lectured on professional and personal development topics, including speaking at the 1995 United Nations conference on the status of women and at Pennsylvania State University's College of Liberal Arts Career Day.

With her husband, Phil Archuletta, she has co-authored *New Mexico Historic Marker Roadmaps: Inspiring Stories of Men, Women, and Places, By the Grace of God: Stories from the American Dreams*, and *Women Marked for History,* which won the New Mexico Heritage Preservation Award in 2015. Rosanne holds an MA from Naropa University and a BA from the Pennsylvania State University.

Rosanne expanded her services in 2019 to include The Dream Benefit™ program, assisting individuals or small groups in identifying and achieving life-enriching personal and professional goals.

### To learn more, visit:
### www.TheDreamBenefit.com

# I Just Wanted to Dance!

As I raised both arms to the sky, I cried out silently, "You have to help me! God, I can't do this anymore!"

It was 5:00 a.m. when I awoke and left the bedroom of the cabin we rented for a long weekend in late August in Eagles Nest, New Mexico. We planned to spend the day fishing in Red River. My husband loves to fish, and I love to sit beside him in the wilderness reading, writing, and meditating.

My silent outcry took place after I had shut the bedroom door and went into the cabin's rustic living room. It was there where the feeling of despair had overtaken me.

"You have to help me! God, I can't do this anymore!" The hopelessness that rushed over me as I silently screamed these words had nothing to do with my surroundings or our plan for a peaceful weekend in nature.

My outburst to God was a reflection of the point that I had reached in my lifelong journey of seeking peace with my body. The night before, at a nearby restaurant, I had yet again eaten unhealthy foods and drank one too many glasses of wine causing me to feel unbalanced. Yes, I felt unbalanced when I had wanted to feel vibrant and clear headed.

Once again, my compulsivity and lack of consciousness won over my desired mindfulness. I had been dealing with this issue for over 60 years, and on this August morning, I finally surrendered to God. Of course, I thought I had given my issue to God many times before, but somehow deep within me I knew this time was different. At the moment of my final surrender I was about 50 pounds overweight. I had been heavier than this at times throughout my life. However, now that I was over 65 years old, my health had suddenly seemed so much worse because of the excess weight and lack of consistent vigorous exercise.

I became very aware of my body's overall declining health when I was hospitalized twice with COVID within 18 months. The first time was in March 2020, not long after our governor had shut down our state due to the pandemic. During the first weekend of March, I had attended a conference with 1800 people and Mass at The Cathedral Basilica of St. Francis of Assisi with 1500 people present.

Over a three-week period, my blood oxygen dropped to a dangerous level—60 percent. By the time I entered the emergency room at Presbyterian Hospital in Santa Fe, my left leg was twice the size of my right leg. Without knowing it, I'd developed ten blood clots—seven blood clots were in my left leg and three of them surrounded my heart.

After the tests were complete, the doctor told me, to my horror, "You are very sick. Rosanne, you probably were within two hours of expiring. I'm so glad

**Rosanne, you were within two hours of expiring...**

you're here!" The credit goes to my husband. When I first saw my leg's size, I said, "I'll elevate it. If it doesn't go down I'll go see someone on Monday." Monday was two days away. He said, "Get in the car now. We're not discussing this." He drove the 90 miles from our second home in Mountainair to Santa Fe in less than one hour.

My second hospital visit came at Christmas of the following year. I was diagnosed with COVID pneumonia. Because I have asthma, my condition was critical, yet again. After having to stay on oxygen for two months at home after leaving the hospital, I had recommitted, once again, to creating a much healthier lifestyle. Yet, here I was, eight months later, finally surrendering to God.

Let me share with you how this lifelong war with my body began.

Shocking as this may sound, I was put on my first "doctor diet" when I was three years old. My father, who died in his early 60s, had many bad habits and was at least 40 pounds overweight at the time. He was very concerned about his wife and his four children having weight issues. So, when I began becoming "pudgy" at such a young age, he decided my mother and our family pediatrician had to help me before I became obese. My mom would take me to the pediatrician for a weigh-in every few weeks. I found it ironic that my pediatrician probably was a good 50 pounds overweight himself.

The battle that raged within me throughout my lifetime began.

My mom felt it was wrong that we were doing this, but honestly, she did not have a say in the matter. So, after each weigh-in, no matter if I gained or lost weight, the result was the same: for doing a good job of staying on the limited diet at home, Mom took me to the counter of a local drug store and rewarded me with a milkshake and cheeseburger. I've told this story to therapists over the years. They were all saddened, knowing what a terrible psychological pattern this created within me.

Throughout my childhood I became increasingly self-conscious about my body size. Both of my parents were now fully focused on me and my fluctuating weight. I remember so many painful moments.

One of those moments brings tears to my eyes, even now, as I replay the memory. I remember what it

> **I was so self-conscious about my body I couldn't let myself go and feel free.**

was like when I was six years old and the heaviest girl in tights in my ballet and tap classes. Choreographed dance was something I always enjoyed. Most of the time, I was so self-conscious about my body, I couldn't just let myself go and feel free. Yet, every once in a while, I became one with the music, and it was pure joy! I just wanted to dance!

Another heartbreaking time was when I was eight years old. I was about to take my first holy communion in the Catholic Church. Even with the issues in my life, I always felt close to Jesus and was excited to receive the Eucharist, "His bread of life," for the first time. I had to go to a special dress shop to get my white first communion dress in a plus size. In spite of the fact there was such a fuss made about the dress' size, I loved that beautiful dress.

Then, a few weeks before my first communion, I got the mumps. What a nightmare! My mother was completely freaked out about the way I would look in my photographs—because of the mumps and the weight. She insisted that my "headshot" be done in a way to decrease my double chin. I remember being so embarrassed as she discussed what she wanted with the photographer, speaking to him as if I was not in the room. I know she was trying to protect me, but at the time, I felt so miserable. It was supposed to be a joyous time of my deepening connection to Jesus and my faith; that's what I wanted.

Believe it or not, it was not long after this when I was diagnosed with near-sightedness and was given my first pair of glasses to wear in the second grade. Of course, this added to my self-consciousness even more. I prayed and prayed for help.

By the time I was 12, I had gained more weight. Most days, I felt hopeless when putting on my clothes for the seventh grade. My father began taking doctor prescribed "diet pills." He talked to our family doctor about prescribing them to me, too, in an attempt to get my weight down. The doctor said that they were having good results with teenagers, so the doctor recommended that my dad discuss it with me. What was *not* mentioned at the time, was what can happen when a 12-year-old takes these powerful drugs. Because of my overwhelming desire to lose weight, I was thrilled that my father gave me the prescription. I believed it would save me from this raging battle I was having with my body. Of course, I quickly realized that it wouldn't be that simple.

Due to the sleepless nights caused by the amphetamines, I became out of sorts immediately. In the midst of my ever-present helplessness regarding my body, I still had my God-given gift of an upbeat, positive nature. It seems to me that God had given me a "smile in my soul" to help me through my difficult circumstances. In reaction to the diet pills, I rapidly began going downhill, emotionally. My positive, upbeat nature completely disappeared! To counteract my emotion's reaction to these

> **My positive, upbeat nature completely disappeared.**

pills, I began smoking cigarettes to calm me down. When I think of smoking at such a young age, I am ashamed. God did help me overcome this addiction in my early twenties, and I am grateful!

Over a six-month period, I became very thin. I became so thin that there were comments from people around me about the fact that I looked ill. *What? I thought I was supposed to become beautiful when I was thin!* I became hopeless all over again! Too fat? Too thin? I remember thinking about killing myself. I was so miserable at this point, believing I'd never get to a peaceful relationship with my body. How could I go on?

I decided to take action—I took 20 aspirins, and to my surprise I didn't die! What did happen was that my hearing was severely reduced. After my mom talked to the doctor about my condition, I spent the day dealing with induced vomiting. I was so angry! I was angry at myself for causing this nightmare. My mother was so frightened, and my father was so worried about what would become of me! I had grown up praying to Jesus with my siblings each night at one another's bedsides. I always reached out to Him as my brother when I had nowhere else to go. Now, after my ridiculous suicide attempt, I was even filled with anger toward Jesus. Of course, everyone agreed it was time that I was taken off of the diet pills, and I gained most of the weight back over the following months.

My battle with my body raged on!

As I moved through my high school years, I tried to focus on other things. In spite of my insecurities, because of my outgoing, God-given positive nature, I had many friends and was involved in interesting activities. When many of my friends were trying out for cheerleading, majorettes, and other performance-related pursuits, I decided to find something I thought I could go after, too, even though I was overweight. So, I tried out for color guard. There were many people vying for the position, but my love for choreographed dance was very helpful. For the tryouts, I had to learn a rifle twirling routine, which I accomplished with tremendous focus, will, prayer, and supportive friends. I made the cut and joined my friends at practice and at our performances. I just loved it! Color guard became a bright spot in my life. Afterall, I just wanted to dance!

I graduated and began my freshman year at Penn State, where I found a way to keep my weight somewhat consistent. This was accomplished with the use of cigarettes and a daily low-calorie intake of food. I never really embraced exercise while I was there, but the campus is so large, it was not difficult to be active.

My battle with my body became worse again in my 20s while living in San Francisco. After I was hospitalized with severe asthma when I was 24, I was forced to quit smoking cigarettes. Of course, this caused me to begin to gain weight once again.

I was blessed to find a wonderful church community and a very supportive minister there. I confided in her about the many issues I had at the time. She referred me to a female therapist who was the answer to my prayers at that time. This therapist helped me stabilize my life in many ways. She believed in 12-step programs and recommended that I attend Overeaters Anonymous—the 12-step program for people with food issues.

Living in the Marina district of San Francisco, I started attending meetings there. The Marina is where you see the "beautiful young people." I found those meetings to be very healing. First of all, they were God-centered. They refer to God as the "higher power." In the meetings, I saw many women who I had seen in the Marina's bars and restaurants. They drove beautiful cars and had gorgeous boyfriends. I was envious of the lifestyle I believed they had achieved. Little did I know, so many of them were bulimic or anorexic. The experience of hearing their horrific stories made me feel better. Yes, I wore my ongoing "battle with my body" on the outside; everyone could see my battle. Somehow though, it seemed an improvement over what these women were experiencing. I thanked God for these meetings. And, for a time, I did lose some weight and somewhat stabilized.

Around this time, I made the decision to quit my job and start my own business. Little did I know that this change would restart the battle with my body. I believe this may have been caused by my fear of failure. All I know was that I was thrown into a downward emotional spiral once again.

My prayers were answered when my business began to become very successful, and I found a place that I called "The Farm" in San Diego. This residential program helped me lose weight in a short period of time. I had the money and the time to start going there for

146

two weeks at a time. The program included raw food and wheatgrass and vegetable smoothies, and I did isometric exercises twice a day. *Voila!* I consistently dropped 16 pounds on each visit. *I found my answer! Yes!* I could lose the weight, gain the weight back, and lose the weight again whenever I wanted! I had no concern about the impact this cycle would have on my metabolism. I believed this program was the answer to my prayers. But in reality, the battle raged on!

By the time I left San Francisco and moved to New Mexico, I was feeling good about myself. I was completely dependent on "The Farm," but still didn't realize this was a bad thing. I was exercising more, which felt good. I discovered NIA choreographed exercise, combining dance, martial arts, and yoga. As you know, I just wanted to dance.

When I moved to New Mexico and met my future husband, for a variety of reasons, my trips to "The Farm" stopped. I believed I knew enough to keep going on my own, but my weight became unstable once again. The battle with my body began once more.

My husband "loved me as I am," bringing no attention to my weight fluctuation. We really are soulmates. Even so, his full love and support could not resolve my compulsivity with food and my lack of interest in exercise that began all over again. On some level, I believed that love would conquer all! I felt desperate yet again. If such a loving home couldn't help me break this pattern either, it seemed there was truly no way out.

> **If such a loving home couldn't help me break this pattern either, it seemed there was truly no way out.**

But finally, as I raised my arms to cry out to God that August morning not that long ago, a true miracle happened. About six weeks later, I heard from an old colleague of mine with whom I had not spoken in years. It was October when we reconnected on the phone. He had a senior position at a company that would hire me as a consultant.

We had a friendly conversation about our mutual work, and as the call was ending, he asked if he could share something personal with me. What he shared was shocking. He had lost nearly 100 pounds in 18 months and was nearly off of insulin for the first time in 27 years. He shared how he had discovered an anti-inflammatory diet that had changed his life. Most of the time, he was no longer eating processed foods or anything containing gluten. He was taking probiotic supplements and other vitamins that supported his body's health. Because his testimony was so compelling, I believed this was the answer to the prayer that I held in my heart for over 60 years!

Yes! This new way of living was the final answer to my prayers. I know that I'm finally walking on my personal path to freedom! The battle with my body that had raged on since I was three years old is over! With God's help, I am finally able to declare a ceasefire!

I am continuing to walk through this period of personal transformation. I see my goal weight clearly now, although I'm not obsessed with it. So, for the first time in my life, I believe I will stay the course and reach it.

Now, the final date of reaching my goal is not what's motivating me anymore. I feel empowered as I finish each day, knowing I'm finally taking good care of myself. I am at peace! The battle is truly over! Instead of the constant confrontation with the part of myself that has always been compulsive about food, that voice has become silent. When I see foods that I know will not support the health of my body, I have a new, loving voice in my head. *Yes, that food is there, but it no longer has anything to do with you!* I believe that voice is the Holy Spirit guiding me.

The key was complete surrender. By now, I know I would have left this new lifestyle had it not been for my complete surrender to God. As I review my life and my relationship with food, I realize that many diet programs could have brought me to this place within myself. I had been steadily changing for the better over the years as I turned one issue after another over to God for His help and guidance. But until now, I had not fully turned over my battle with my body to Him. And when I finally did, my life was changed

**The key was complete surrender!**

148

forever! Finally, I can feel joy pulsating through me throughout the day.

After all, I still just want to dance!

## Kari L. Jones,
## author, adventurer,
## Bible teacher

Kari L. Jones, a passionate lover of Jesus, is madly in love with her husband and four children. Adventuring, traveling, exploring, and discovering new places and things with her family fills her joy cup.

Kari is a passionate teacher with a deep desire to equip God's children to advance the Kingdom, draw others closer to the Father's heart and glorify His name. She strongly believes that every person is created for a unique and powerful purpose and has a strong, impactful, solution-bringing movement inside of them waiting to be ignited for the Kingdom here on earth. Kari gets excited about seeing people become empowered to be and accomplish what they were made for.

In 2022, Kari published her first book, *My Unboxed Heart: Breaking Free from the Bondages of an Emotionally Abusive Mother*, hoping to encourage others who've been emotionally abused that they're not alone and give them tools to heal.

Learn more now at:

**www.KariLJones.com**

# Wallflower to Warrior

To all the wallflowers who secretly come alive while waging war on the world's greatest evils…usually only in the comfort of their imagination. They feel the pain of a slow, silent, and unseen death of the soul as their inner warrior falls grossly short of an acceptable outward life experience. Both warrior feet are stuck in the thick, cement-like mud from the pressure to live a compliant, "sweet," "good," "Christian" life, and the mud feels stronger than the overwhelming agony of not unleashing the warrior within.

This is for every person who has shared my struggle with the inner tug-of-war between the person they feel created to be and the person they feel *conditioned* to be. The raging fear of hurting and being rejected by loved ones seems to win the daily battle rather than the fear of not fulfilling our divinely ordained purpose. Many days are spent on the verge of tears—our failure to fear God rather than people haunts us. Many times, we are misunderstood.

For me, feeling the presence of the Lord, interacting with the Holy Spirit, and being aware of the spiritual atmosphere was always normal. However, what was just as real to me as the physical realm was not accepted or understood by those closest to me growing up. I had no one to guide me, instruct me, council me, or comfort me as a child in this area. This resulted in so many conflicting and confusing thoughts about who I was and how I was supposed to fit into society.

As a little girl, I remember feeling Jesus come into my room at night and kiss me on the cheek. I remember feeling completely at peace, loved, and safe, knowing Jesus Himself was watching over me. When I told my mom of Jesus visiting me, it was brushed off as either a dream or my imagination. When I strongly sensed something not right in the atmosphere, I would try to communicate the best I knew how, only to be misunderstood and told I was being ridiculous, called judgmental, or accused of being too sensitive. These occurrences led me to conclude something was wrong with me. *Why can't I blindly and effortlessly participate in all aspects of life without a care in the world like others seem to be able to?*

I remember one time, around middle school age, I was reading my Bible on my bed as I often did. I loved reading the Bible. This particular time, I was reading in 1 Corinthians and had one of my first, to my memory, revelations. The Holy Spirit literally came upon me, highlighting verse

> **I was misunderstood —told I was being ridiculous, judgmental, or too sensitive.**

4:10, "We are fools for Christ, but you are so wise in Christ! We are weak, but you are strong! You are honored, we are dishonored!" The words "I am a fool for Christ" went on repeat in my head. Then, I started to say those words out loud: "I am a fool for Christ." As I spoke, a deep sense of understanding came over me. My entire being was filled with joy, and I loved what I was experiencing! I was called to be His, to belong and to serve Jesus with all that I am. To the world I was going to look very foolish, but that was more than okay; I was excited to be the fool for Christ.

For the first time in my memory, I became so filled with overwhelming joy and excitement with this new living understanding of the Scriptures. This gave clarity to my identity and pierced through the confusion. I just had to tell someone—this was how excited I was. Running out of my room and down the hall, I was looking for anyone to share this revelation with. I found my mom working in the kitchen, and with a great big grin on my face and my body shaking with excitement, I blurted out, "I am a fool for Christ!"

My mother sharply turned toward me and sternly replied, "We do not talk like that in this house." I stood there baffled, not sure how to respond. I literally just had an encounter with the Living God whose Holy Spirit led me into a revelation of His Holy Word, and I was being scolded for sharing. I was growing up in what I knew to be a "Christian" home. My parents religiously took our family to church every Sunday and believed the Bible to be true, so I wasn't understanding the problem. I must have looked completely confused by her reaction because my mother repeated herself. When I finally replied, I remember saying, "But that is what the Bible says." I proved it using my Bible, and my mother's response was, "Well, that is not how I take it. And we will not talk like that in this house."

I tried to explain my revelation, but she would not hear it. Her response felt like a muzzle, silencing me from sharing with anyone. Walking back to my room confused, I wondered, *who am I?* Every time I felt as if I began to head down a path to discover my purpose and identity, I felt disassembled back to pieces without an instruction manual to put them together.

Unfortunately, this was not an isolated event. Revelations of Scripture, dreams, visions, Holy Spirit encounters, hearing the voice of God, prophecy, praying in the Spirit, speaking God's Word, everything that made me feel normal, alive, joy filled, excited, and fulfilling my purpose, seemed *unacceptable*. This deepened my confusion about my identity and purpose. Trying to "fit in" and be who I felt I was supposed to be made life miserable. Being myself, I felt despised, bullied, and shamed. Trying to find middle ground made me feel fake. *Will the confusion ever stop and will I find my place in this world?*

Let me give you some more backstory. I grew up in a middle-class home with my mom, dad, brother, and sister. On the outside, I lacked nothing; all my physical needs were met, my parents were happily married, and we attended church regularly. However, I still hungered for more spiritually and emotionally.

I was being conditioned to fit into the same system my parents grew up in; the only system they knew. They created a home environment that was physically safe, controlled, and predictable. I was being trained to be a good hard-working, law-abiding citizen who positively contributed to society while attending church and representing Christ with a sweet, loving attitude. We volunteered and helped those less fortunate than us. We were good people who went to church, but I couldn't see what else separated us from the world. Real, transformative Holy Spirit power was missing—just a lot of motions and routine. Inside, I craved more.

Always knowing I wanted to be used by God in great ways, throughout my childhood I would imagine myself as a missionary in foreign lands being used by God to bring healings, miracles, and saving souls by the masses. I desired to be in the middle of a great revival, unashamed and unyielding to the world. I wanted to have personal testimonies of fire falling from heaven, rivers parting, and the dead being raised. Everything the Bible offered and more was what I wanted to experience. I had so much faith and desire for this I thought I would explode from keeping it in. Unfortunately, hiding these dreams was necessary.

The filling and moving of the Spirit amongst crowds were only things I'd read about but never experienced. *Why isn't everyday life laced with the tangible power of the Holy Spirit?* These things seemed to only happen in past times or faraway lands. Any outward expression for my deep desire to experience the Spirit of God were casually treated, not excitedly supported. So, I learned to keep it to myself. I felt I had to be cautious in sharing my desires, revelations, dreams, and any small private encounters with the Lord. There seemed to be no room for the Spirit in my childhood home, and therefore, I felt there was no room for *me*.

> There seemed to be no room for the Spirit in my childhood home, and therefore, I felt there was no room for me.

As a child filled with passion and a wildness, my parents worked hard to tame and train me to be—who they felt would be—an acceptable, successful contributor to the comfortable societal system they knew. Their training methods would leave me lost, confused, and emotionally wounded. I couldn't wait for the day I could move out, break free from the controlled and suffocating environment, and finally discover my true identity while seeking the fullness of God. The exhausting, sabotaging experience of being forced into a box I was never meant to fit into—the silent, complying nobody—was something I no longer wanted.

Growing up, I could sense something wasn't right with my relationship with my parents. I knew this because I hated always feeling defeated around my mom and invisible to my dad. Feeling I had to compete for their attention, I became angry with them for not seeing me and accepting me for who I was. *What does being loved feel like? I'm not sure...* I was lost, suffering from emotional pain so strongly it dictated the way I lived. Yet I felt so ashamed by my pain since there wasn't any tangible abuse or traumatic event to blame for my emotional disorientation. They raised me the only way they knew how, and as a result, they did not realize they were forcing me into a box I wasn't designed for. I felt tolerated and not celebrated.

Going to church once a week, silently and respectfully sitting on a pew for an hour, and then living as the sweet, "good" Christian girl the rest of the week wasn't satisfying. I had too much passion in me for that kind of life. Until I could figure out how to translate what I felt on the inside to be my outward experience, I took a place on the wall of the church and became one of its many wallflowers. There I stayed for many years, allowing the words spoken to me and over me to turn into lies that *no one wants to hear me, no one wants to see me, and I am unworthy.* This kind of identity is lonely and depressing.

In my early twenties, after returning from a year of serving in China, my childhood church invited me to share a testimony of my time there. I was excited. Teaching and giving testimony of the Lord is at the heart of who I am. Many from the church came, including my dad. I hoped this would be the moment my dad would see my gifting, my heart, who God created me to be, and begin shifting his perspective to be a supportive, parental figure in my life. I hoped this would be a pivotal moment in our relationship, so I excitedly and enthusiastically shared.

After an hour or so, I finished, completely energized and overflowing with joy. *This is what I was born for—drawing others closer to God through teaching and sharing of His goodness.* The response from the audience was encouraging. The hope in me swelled as I awaited my dad's feedback. As the audience dissipated, my dad stepped forward.

"What did you think?" I eagerly asked.

"You were a little preachy," was all he ever said about what I shared. *Crushing.* I wanted more, but he wouldn't give it. I thought I openly and honestly shared my prayerfully prepared testimony. *God, if my delivery was wrong, please change it,* was my heart's cry.

Soon after, another local church invited me to share for their morning service; with God's leading, I accepted. I invited my parents, craving their support. They refused. When I asked why, they responded, "We've already heard all you have to say." Even though the response from the church's congregation was overwhelmingly positive, with members sharing the impact of my words years later, my parents' actions, as unintentional as they may have been, made me feel this expression of myself was unacceptable. Even though there were pockets of people who encouraged me in who God created me to be, the approval I sought was that of my parents. But thankfully, something changed.

Epiphanes and sudden ah-ha moments are not a huge part of my story. It has all been in the journey—following the breadcrumbs of the Lord, reflecting, surrendering, seeking, listening, and choosing the change. The emotional abuse I experienced as a child and young adult formed massive, deep wounds in my heart, leading me to believe lies about myself and paralyzing me from living the passionate life I felt deep in my spirit. Emotional strongholds that formed from a series of intangible events were hard to express, hard to pinpoint. I hesitated to seek help from others because when I tried to verbalize my brokenness, it was too easily dismissed

A pivotal moment in my thinking occurred one Sunday after church when I was a teenager. Standing in the foyer, off to the side against the wall, I was waiting for my mother to be done visiting so we could go home. I wasn't talking to anyone, I just stood there, doing my wallflower duty as I often did on Sundays. An older lady in the congregation approached me and said, "How does it make you feel?" I was first surprised she was talking to me—because she didn't normally—and then confused by the question. I replied, "Excuse me?" This older lady repeated the question with more clarity, "How does it make you feel…the way your mother treats you?" I was shocked. For the first time, someone was acknowledging what I had been feeling. Not knowing how to answer, I just said, "I don't know."

This elder church goer ended our little interaction sharing that she "sees" me and has seen the way my mother treats me. I didn't speak to that woman much before and not much after this interaction, but I know God sent her to approach me that day.

From that Sunday forward, God led people into my life who acted as guideposts and breadcrumbs, directing me to the truth I needed to discover.

The turnaround has been a slow journey of peeling back the layers of my conditioned mind, revealing and acknowledging the lies, and replacing them with truth. I struggled for many years to fully trust God and follow His leading off the wall and out of the shadows. My inner critic frequently compared my life to those who've lived through more traumatic experiences. *They've had it much worse.* Shame would envelop me for, what I thought was, unexplainable brokenness. *Lie.*

In following my patient Heavenly Father, He led me to a revelation that changed me forever: *Brokenness comes from not functioning in the divine order of My original design. To truly get unstuck, divorce the wallflower identity and begin to live in the authority of My purpose for you, Kari.* It was crucial I understood how I was created to function.

In 1 Thessalonians 5:23, we see God's divine order: "Now, may the God of peace and harmony set you apart, making you completely holy. And may your entire being—**spirit, soul, and body**—be kept completely flawless in the appearing of our Lord Jesus, the Anointed One." The order here is not random but of great significance; it gave the explanation I needed for my brokenness.

The spirit is the part of me that communicates with God. My soul holds my emotions, thoughts, and will. My body is my physical flesh. The spirit is first, then soul, and then body. I was created to function in this particular order. Trying to live in any other order meant I was *out of order.* When I did so, my being was in chaos and I was broken.

When God called me off of the wall, He revealed I had partnered with lies. I allowed those lies to influence how I thought about myself, resulting in a false identity being formed. I believed these lies because

I was operating out of my wounded soul, my thoughts, feelings, and emotions. I was not living from my spirit communing with God and not allowing His truth to influence my emotions—which would affect my actions. I needed to allow God to expose the lies, acknowledge I had been lied to, repent for believing the lies, and forgive those who communicated those lies to me through either words or actions.

> **I needed the lies exposed, to acknowledge I'd been lied to, repent for believing lies, and to forgive.**

The Lord led me to take a momentous action step one morning on a hill by a small chapel. With people walking below, God asked me to shout the name of Jesus. With my heart pounding, I ignored fear of embarrassment, rejection, and judgment and unleashed the warrior. Consciously thrusting everything within me, I did a mighty, unapologetic roar for all to hear: "JESUS!"

Reflecting on the journey, I see God's fingerprints and gentle whispers—evidence that He's led me in His perfect way all along. If the change from wallflower to warrior had been instantaneous (as I would've liked), I would have missed out on the character development, organic relationship growth, strength and endurance building, and many valuable lessons learned along the way. God has graciously been leading, equipping, and teaching me to step into my God-given authority as a warrior through intimacy with Him.

I can choose whether or not I will live out of my spirit communing with God or out of how I feel. Choices are powerful. Making the choice to operate from a place of intimacy with God with my spirit takes practice. I have had to choose to be kind to myself as I learn to operate in this new order. As I grow in my relationship with God through my spirit, I am renewing my mind to align with the Word of God—*truth*.

In this new order, I can now see my parents through a different lens. It is not their fault they didn't accept me, validate my calling, understand my giftings, or see the powerful purpose I was designed for. They, like so many, have been conditioned to perform and keep to a specific way of doing things. They did the absolute best they could with what they knew. Even though I did not receive from them what I felt I needed as a child and young adult, that time is not lost. God will use all this to glorify His name. There is purpose in the pressing and the pain I endured. Joseph—who was sold into slavery by his own brothers—may not have initially understood why God placed him in a family who hated him. As part of a divine plan, there was purpose in all of Joseph's pain and suffering. Every skill learned, every moment he chose to serve God rather than man or himself, was later used to position Joseph to save the very family that rejected him.

Today my life is in the middle of an epic metamorphosis; one imperfect action step after another has me chasing after more understanding and revelation knowledge of who my Creator is and who I am in Him. The muzzle has been torn off and my voice is now surrendered for the use of Almighty God. My voice is His—strong, determined, and unwavering to the opinions of others. This divine transformation is fueled by prioritizing spending time soaking in God's presence.

For every person who has felt overlooked and silenced, the time is now for our great awakening. Each of us who responds to God's call will be anointed, empowered, equipped, strengthened, and encouraged. Our Creator designed us to be radical, unafraid, bold, and powerful! Surrendered to the ways of God, we will be the unyielding, uncompromised, and unashamed shock waves God can use to influence history. We will reject all redefinitions of our identity. We are only who God says we are.

In reality, we were never wallflowers because in God's church, there are no walls. Our warrior awakening frees us from the lies that chained us to the artificial wall. Our healing comes when we see who we really are through living from our spirit in communion with God. Finally, our purpose is to walk with God, advancing His Kingdom, drawing people closer to Him and glorifying His name! It's time!

> **We are only who God says we are!**

## Liz Jack,
### entrepreneur, coach, speaker

Being a West Texas Cowgirl, Liz Jack grew up understanding the value of loving Jesus, family, and was raised to have a strong work ethic. Liz is an entrepreneur and owns Allied Allegiance, a company that helps people with gold and silver investments, affordable healthcare alternatives, and helping business owners to increase revenue. She has successfully coached large teams of people and has been a motivational speaker for various events. Currently she hosts a weekly radio spot called "My Best Life" that airs every Sunday morning at 7:30 a.m. Central on Western Heritage Radio (judyjames.com).

Liz and her husband, Greg, live right outside of Amarillo, Texas. They have five grown children and eight grand babies. She is active in her church and has a passion to see people set free from bondage and to succeed and live their best life.

### For more information, check out Liz's website at:

## www.AlliedAllegiance.com

# CHAPTER SIXTEEN
## Liz Jack

# Beauty for Ashes

One day you are on top of the world living your best life, and then within seconds your world is flipped upside down and nothing is ever the same again. Grief finds all of us at some point in life. The question is, how are you going to walk through it?

It was a cold, blustery winter day in Amarillo, Texas, and I was sitting by the crackling fireplace in my living room, smiling because of an "ah-ha" moment. My life was at the best place it had ever been up until then. I had a wonderful husband, David, who loved and adored me and my two children, Austin and Casey. David was a strong Christian man (something I had always prayed for) and he spiritually led our home. He had a good job with the railroad as an engineer, and even though I worked, he financially took good care of us. But the thing I was most thankful for was that I knew I could trust him. When we had married seven months prior, he had meant every word of his vows "to always be there for us." I was married to my best friend; someone I could laugh and grow old with which was something I'd never had before. My heart was overwhelmed with gratitude. *This is the way marriage is supposed to be.*

David and I met through a mutual friend. He was 39 and I was 30, and our friendship quickly led to a deep, meaningful relationship, six months of dating, and then a simple ceremony. He had been married once before, and I had been married twice. My first marriage was to my kids' dad and the second was to Dr. Jekyll and Mr. Hyde— a very abusive and toxic relationship. So, for David and me, this wasn't our first rodeo. We knew what we wanted out of our relationship. We had vowed and prayed on a daily basis to have a relationship that would honor God and would provide Austin and Casey a loving home to grow up in.

For two years, David, Austin, Casey, and I built great memories

161

together—praying and going to church, working, laughing, cooking, taking trips, exercising, bicycling, walking the dog, and building a life. One of the fun memories that comes to mind is when David took Casey (when she was in first grade) out in a dirt field in his old brown Jeep and taught her to drive. My little girl was so proud of herself; she took us all for a drive in the dirt field later and told us about the pretend city and streets they had created and the obstacles she had to drive around. The second memory that makes me laugh was the Saturday morning when I woke up and caught David driving his Jeep next to the sidewalk with a long rope hanging out of the window, and guess what (who) was on the end of the rope? Austin with his skates, being pulled down the sidewalk! The guys knew that when I caught them, it would be the end of that. Of course, they snickered as I scolded them both and lectured them how dangerous that could have been. We were happy. The kids were happy. We were living the dream, and our life was right on course.

Prior to meeting David, my life had been a series of unhealthy relationships regarding men. My mom and dad had divorced when I was young, so I did not grow up experiencing or knowing what a healthy marriage should look like. Even though they were both great people, they just had unresolved problems, and dad's continual absence led to my parents' divorce. My mom was the rock of our family and my dad was always the "fun" parent. Mom was the one who kept the train on the track; she kept us in church and taught us a strong work ethic. Dad trained racehorses and was always traveling to different tracks to race. Even though I knew he loved me, there was always something inside yearning for more time with him.

After many moves and attending five different high schools, I graduated at age 17, moved away, and began Tarleton State University in Stephenville, Texas. This is where I met and later married my first husband at age 19. Looking back, I realize my first husband and I both came from divorced families, and I think we were both trying to "right a wrong" from our childhoods. We simply didn't know how to have a healthy marriage. I am grateful for our two beautiful kids and am happy to say we have become friends. Husband number two should have never been…and quickly became what I call the darkest five years of my life, laden with verbal and physical abuse and infidelity. By the time I divorced for the second time, I was emotionally deflated, embarrassed, and felt like a big failure. I was convinced I would never experience a loving, fulfilling, godly marriage.

My only saving grace was the Word of God hidden deep inside of me from childhood—from all the times my mother made me go to church. As much as the devil lied to me, God's truth would say, "I love you, Liz, and I have a plan and a purpose for you, and it is good." It was God who continued to show me His love, and it was God who was always there, despite the divorces, continually reminding me there is no condemnation in Christ.

> **God was always there, reminding me there is no condemnation in Christ.**

When I met David, I was in a war, battling the lies of the devil, loss, feelings of not being good enough, and unworthiness. Every day David spoke words of encouragement to me and pointed me to Christ. He continually prayed over me which was the sweetest gift a husband can give to his wife, and I was growing emotionally stronger every day. But every once in a while, I would get in my own head and my faith would dwindle. The devil would whisper and say, "You will lose everyone you ever love." That was the stronghold lie that played over and over in my head. God knew the desires of my heart to have a strong, patient, Christian man to partner with and to have a godly marriage with. David and I spent many hours talking about God's truth, being intentional about protecting our marriage and living our best life. Isaiah 61:1-3 is a favorite scripture passage of mine; they are the words God used to carry me through:

"The Spirit of the Sovereign Lord is on me, because the Lord has anointed me to proclaim good news to the poor. He has sent me to bind up the brokenhearted, to proclaim freedom for the captives and release from darkness for the prisoners, to proclaim the year of the Lord's favor and the day of vengeance of our God, to comfort all who mourn and provide for those who grieve in Zion, to bestow on them a crown of beauty instead of ashes, the oil of joy instead of mourning, and a garment of praise instead of a spirit of despair. They will be called oaks of righteousness, a planting of the Lord for the display of his splendor."

I had been in bondage to my thoughts, but then God revealed His truth to me. It set me free and healed me from my past, and I know if He did it for me, He will do it for you.

Two years after we were married, on a Sunday morning in July, is a day I will never forget. Typically we were all hustling to get ready to go to church, but I had an aerobic workshop that day, and David had a headache so he decided he would stay home with the kids. We had all had oatmeal and fruit together for breakfast. The kids were watching cartoons and David went into the bathroom to take a shower. I practiced the exercise routine for a bit, then wanted to say goodbye before I left. When I walked into the bathroom, I found him lying on the floor unconscious. "Austin! Get the phone and come back to the room and call 911!" I yelled to my son. I wouldn't let him inside the bathroom, but I heard him on the phone talking to 911 as I did CPR.

The paramedics showed up quickly and took over CPR, then they ushered me out of the room. The kids and I knelt down and prayed together like we had never prayed before. When the neighbors heard the sirens and saw the ambulance, they came over and took the kids so I could follow the ambulance to the hospital. That previous week, David had gone to the doctor because he wasn't feeling good, and the doctor had sent him to a cardiologist. Little did we know that his aortic valve was slowly tearing.

Here is where the story gets blurry because this is where I went into shock. After about an hour of being at the hospital, someone walked into the room where I was waiting and told me David didn't make it. He had died of an aortic aneurysm. I tried to stand up but the room was spinning, and I fell backward, sobbing uncontrollably in disbelief. I remember trying to compose myself to call his parents, asking them to come to the hospital.

My friends brought the kids to me at the hospital, and I remember a lot of people from church coming to comfort us, too. For several weeks our home was filled with family and friends filling in the gaps—preparing meals, visiting, cleaning—but to tell you the truth, other than making sure my kids were okay, I don't remember much. This is where the fog set in. Somehow, I made funeral arrangements, picked out a casket, and worked through all the

**This is where the fog set in.** details. Somehow, I got up each day, breathed in and out, took care of my kids, and several weeks later, went back to work. Somehow, I continued to go through my day physically, but emotionally I had checked out. *This is too much to handle!*

I have read that there are at least six stages to grief: shock, denial, anger, bargaining, depression, and finally, acceptance. I can tell you there is no certain pattern, but you *have to* go through grief or else it will trap you, keep you in bondage, and leave you bitter. It will leave you in the prison of misery that Isaiah 61 talks about. At first, I ping-ponged back and forth between denial and anger. I would see someone in the store who looked like David or reminded me of him and would have a nervous breakdown there in the store, uncontrollably crying. On several occasions I abandoned full shopping carts in the aisle. My mind still wouldn't accept he had died. I continually had dreams about him. My mind did everything it could to bring him back to life, but every day I would wake up and relive his death all over again. I wavered in this stage for over a year.

My next emotion was anger; this was an emotion I could operate in. I would get mad at God, thinking *what kind of God would take away my husband when I was finally happy?* To deal with the anger, I began running, which is interesting because it's something I had never been fond of before. I would run and run and run until I physically couldn't run anymore, drenched in sweat, as if I could out run all of my emotions. The anger would continue to show up again and again, and I would find myself thinking *I cannot trust God with my happiness.* This made me lay another brick to the wall of self-protection around my heart.

Then, I got mad at David for dying and would rant at him for leaving me. It's funny now, but David never wanted us to fry any food inside of the house because of the smell. So, he had an electric fryer set up in the garage. I used to tease him and tell him I was going to fry fish on top of his '69 Camaro. So, one day when I was mad at him for dying, I went to the store, bought two pounds of bacon, and fried it all up in the kitchen. As I cooked, I ranted and raved, asking him what he was going to do about it.

Next came the depression; I simply missed him and didn't know how to handle my feelings. In front of the kids, I had to fake a smile, be the encourager, and comfort them, and at work I had to hold my head up high and do my job. But when I was alone, I was a mess and full of unresolved pain. I had always had trouble sleeping well, but the grief left me unable to sleep at all. My doctor prescribed Ambien, and it would knock me out and helped me sleep, but it opened up another dark door of chemical dependency which took over 12 years for me to get free from.

The first year after David's death was the hardest. Every holiday, his birthday, our anniversary, etc., was a reminder that my future did not include him—a reminder that I would never get to spend another day with him. That reminder compounded with the fact that I had experienced my mom and dad's divorce, two divorces of my own, and now David dying. Two years earlier, my grandad died in front of me, then fast forward several years after David's death when my dad unexpectedly died at age 64. My brother and I had to make the difficult decision to pull him off of life support. The devil was reaffirming the lie: *I will lose everyone I ever love!*

> **Unresolved pain manifests in strange ways.**

Unresolved pain manifests in strange ways. For the next several years after David's death, I tried to cope in various ways—from drowning myself in work, dating to alleviate loneliness before I was emotionally ready, living in severe pain, which was later labeled as fibromyalgia, to quitting my job, and homeschooling my kids. Homeschooling I took very seriously, and it was one of the best decisions I made. It gave me much-needed quality time with my kids and helped us grow closer than ever. Even though my decisions weren't always the best, I always kept us in church, knowing Christ was our anchor.

Isaiah 61:1-3 talks about beauty for ashes. In order to get to the beauty, something has to burn. Ashes are what's left after something has died. For me, I had to die to myself, soulish thoughts, control, and doing things based on my emotions. I had to learn to walk by His Spirit and lean not on my own understanding. Learning to trust God was a big one. I prayed, pleaded, and fought for my emotional freedom. I read every book I could get my hands on about freedom and clung to scriptures such as Galatians 5:1, which says, "It is for freedom that Christ has set us free. Stand firm then, and do not let yourselves be burdened again by a yoke of slavery."

One of the most powerful book studies I did was Neil Anderson's book, *The Bondage Breakers*. It taught me how to break and destroy wrong mindsets and how to replace those lies with God's Word. So, I surrounded myself with strong, Christian prayer warriors who were more mature in Christ than I was. Today, I have an army of women who encourage me to press into God and live His truth. Find your army, my friends. They'll fight for you.

For healing from a broken heart, the only remedy I know is God and time. Verses 2 and 3 of Isaiah 61 say:

"...to comfort all who mourn and provide for those who grieve in Zion, to bestow on them a crown of beauty instead of ashes, the oil of joy instead of mourning, and a garment of praise instead of a spirit of despair. They will be called oaks of righteousness, a planting of the Lord for the display of his splendor."

Over time, God took my pain and used it for His glory. God has since opened up doors for me to minister and encourage others who have experienced grief. I am only able to do this because I have walked in their shoes and can testify how God has healed me, redeemed me, and has given me beauty for ashes. Now I know Him at deeper levels because of the tragedy He carried me through.

A lot of life happened during the ten years after David died; my kids became young adults and went off to college. I had finally learned to be comfortable and healthy on my own. Emotionally I was in a good place but knew I needed a career change. The health and fitness industry was not generating the income I wanted. Knowing I needed to plan better for my financial future, I found a school and became a licensed Insurance Adjuster. Shortly after I got my license, the BP oil spill took place, and I took an assignment in Louisiana. It was a big change leaving Amarillo and heading to Hammond, Louisiana, to do something I had never done before. But I had prayed and God had answered; I knew I was supposed to go.

As I was driving from Texas to Louisiana, a radio program featured the famous scripture from the book of Esther: *for such a time as this*. Then, I saw it on a billboard. Then, a friend of mine gave me a bracelet inscribed with *"For such a time as this"* and knew I was headed in the direction God wanted me to go. For the next year and a half, I endured the toughest job I had ever done, working over 12 hours a day and going 3.5 months before having a day off.

Ten months into the project, I met Greg Jack from Baton Rouge, Louisiana. He was a friend of a friend and was also working on the BP oil spill project. Neither one of us were looking for a relationship, but we instantly connected. Our time together consisted of talking and walking during coffee breaks and lunch and eventually led to dinner and seeing each other every day. On our second date, I remember telling Greg that God came first in my life and if he had a problem with that, we didn't need to see each other anymore. He chuckled and said, "No, I don't have a problem with that." After 3.5 months of dating, he took me to his family camp on the coast and proposed. He said God told him one day after he went home from work to marry me, and who was he to argue with God?

We have spent 12 wonderful years of marriage together, and I pray we have many more ahead. I can tell you the devil no longer has a foothold to lie to me about losing him. We will all die at some point, and time and life is full of change, but I refuse to stop living. The lessons I have

**The devil no longer has a foothold to lie to me.**

learned are that we should live each day as if it were our last. We should tell our family and friends we love them. We should put our hope in Jesus and know He is our constant.

Grief is something we will all walk through. We are not guaranteed tomorrow. It has taught me to appreciate each and every day and to have a mindset of gratitude instead of loss. I have learned that if we keep our eyes on Jesus, He will carry us through tragedy and pain and will give us beauty for ashes. We will become those Oaks of Righteousness, a planting of the Lord for the display of His splendor.

"…that they may be called trees of righteousness, the planting of the Lord, that He may be glorified." —Isaiah 61:3

## Andy Bunch, author, life and writing coach, entrepreneur

In the footsteps of Hemingway and London, Andy Bunch is an adventure writer. He built a church in Mexico, sang for his supper in Canada, taught archery in Alaska, and studied history in the UK. He's trained in martial arts and once spent a week in the woods with only a knife, flint, and black plastic.

Since completing his BS in business, Andy has become a Certified Kingdom Entrepreneur Coach, Life Purpose Coach, and Grief Recovery Specialist. In 2021 Andy was honored with ordination by his home church.

Andy is currently a professional copywriter and has been writing for 30 years. He has published six books under his own name and ghost written many more. His passion project is helping Christian writers reach convergence (where their unique nature, experience, talent, and passion all align with God's purpose for them).

Andy loves to speak on the topic of "Authentic Identity for Creatives" and is currently building a system of organization to help creatives reduce stress, create more, and earn income while having Impact. What others are saying about Andy:

"A shout out to Andy Bunch for helping me move forward with a career decision. Andy helped me gain clarity on what was holding me back from moving forward." —Lynette Randall

"I want to thank Andy for helping me get a major breakthrough in discovering my field of favor and understanding the people I should serve." —Alex Morozov

## Connect with Andy more via these sites:

Websites: **christianwritersdojo.com/pro-bio**
Books: **sirbunch.com/sir-bunch-author/my-books/**
LinkedIn: **www.linkedin.com/in/sirbunch/**
Facebook: **www.facebook.com/TaleScribe**

# CHAPTER SEVENTEEN
## Andy Bunch

# New Expectations

Growing up I always felt there were two kinds of sin: Type one included Original Sin and the sins we didn't mean to do because we didn't know any better. Those were sins Jesus died for. Type two sins were the things we walked into with eyes wide open. Those were the sins I still felt like I had to do *my* part to fix. I don't know where the idea came from, but it was always there.

Feeling like a ship adrift at sea as I grew up, it was like there was one vital part missing, one part to complete the repair in order to charge full-steam ahead. But what was that missing piece? *So much potential…and so lost, drifting.* I was confused, frustrated, and felt like I didn't belong—at school and even in my own family at times. Something in me said *you are made for more*, yet something else said *but you'll never find it*. Let me give you some backstory.

My paternal grandparents were farmers and college professors. My granddad had two doctorate degrees—one in math and one in science. He milked cows at 5 a.m., then taught college all day, came home, milked the cows again, and graded papers until he went to bed. My grandmother had a masters in home economics and taught high school.

My dad was a genius and an inventor whose parents were disappointed that he stopped at a BS in engineering. He met and married my mother in college and went straight to work as an electrical engineer, where he worked for 30 years.

Mom was punished severely by her mother for every mistake, even things her siblings did. Miraculously, she didn't become abusive herself, but the message to her was that the world was inherently unsafe and unforgiving. The slightest misstep could be your last. My father was her hero.

When I was four and wanted to jump in mud puddles, my mom

told me they were bottomless and I would get sucked all the way through the Earth. When my older cousin threw me in the creek on a hot day, I freaked out because I was pretty sure I was entering a vortex that would pull me to my doom. *My body will wash up in China somewhere.*

Despite her imaginative stories, Mom always told me I was destined for greatness like my father. The challenge was how much Dad traveled for work; he was often gone. I felt like I was on my own to figure out just where and how to be great.

> **Mom always told me I was destined for greatness like my father.**

Before I entered school, my family moved to a tiny farmhouse on a remote patch of land with a river running across it. I think Dad bought it for cash when he sold our big house in town. The original farmhouse had one bedroom, but someone had enclosed the front porch to make another. We had one bathroom for the five of us, a party-line phone, and no TV. My teenage sisters thought they were in hell, and my mother got really depressed from the isolation.

I, however, loved it. I went feral. I would strip to my underwear and run in the woods with my trusty Collie, Lad, until the sun went down. I fished and hunted imaginary monsters with my real bow. I wanted to grow up to be Daniel Boone.

We heated the place with a woodstove, so my dad would take me out on the weekends to cut wood. We had fruit trees and a large truck garden, and in the winter, the frost would form thick on the inside of the single-pane windows.

When Dad was in town, he read books by the fire at night. He probably read 100 books a year. I sat in his lap and tried my best to unjumble the letters on the page. Reading was hard for me, but I wanted to *be* that book.

After our first year there, we'd settled into things. My dad continued to invent things like a burglar alarm that would go off before you actually touched it and a carburetor that ran on flour. He successfully patented a system to locate downed power lines in remote areas. Dad abandoned each invention at some point as "impractical," but he was repeatedly promoted, eventually reaching NW Regional

DC Expert. I did my own scientific experiments. I once mixed a bunch of household cleaners in the shampoo bottle and dyed my sister's hair red. In my defense, it did get her hair clean.

My sisters continued to hate living there. My oldest sister, who was eight years older than me, escaped to boarding school. When she came home on holiday break, she was so bored she wanted us to clean the house. I wanted to play. She decided I was lazy and never really changed her mind. My mom just told her, "He's not like you, sweetheart." The lesson I learned is that my family placed great value on being industrious.

When I was seven, they finally put me in a school. Our property was between school districts and neither bus came near us, but we convinced one of them to do it, so that's the school I ended up attending.

I didn't enjoy school, and it didn't like me much either. I was one of four students in my class who wasn't Native American. The four of us were bullied pretty hard, and it wasn't easy to play together after school since we all lived far apart.

My poor grades didn't go unnoticed. When my dad was in town he tried to be encouraging. "You have plenty of time to improve things; just try to keep up, because it gets harder from here."

One evening forever lives in my memory. As our family sat together eating dinner, my dad asked my oldest sister what she wanted to be when she grew up.

"An accountant or a schoolteacher," she answered. My middle sister answered that she wanted to be a wife and mother.

When it was my turn to answer, my mom was no doubt worried I'd say I wanted to be Robin Hood or something, so she added, "You can be anything you want, and we'll be proud of you. Even if you are a garbage man, as long as you are happy and making the most of your talents."

I responded boldly, "I want to write books."

My dad made a face, and my mom blurted out, "But you could be a garbage man!"

"Why do you want me to be a garbage man?" I asked.

"Well, it's just that you need to do something that makes money, or you won't be able to have a family."

My dad added, "Most writers aren't famous until after they die. I mean it's hard to make a living doing that."

I was stunned. *What was I supposed to be great at if not writing books?*

Mom tried to help. "It's just that you can't spell. I'd hate to see you try to do something you have no skill at."

From then on, I wondered how I was going to achieve greatness. Being an author was all I wanted. *What else could I possibly do?* Everyone was sure I would be smart like my dad, but my grades said otherwise, and my parents were pretty sure I could do more if I tried. The problem was, I *was* trying.

One summer, my family volunteered to host girls from my sister's boarding school for Vacation Bible School (VBS). Volunteers would come to work the VBS event to earn money off their private school bill.

One of the VBS girls we hosted was overweight and awkward, age thirteen, with curly red hair and bad acne. At our house we still didn't have TV, so we played games and read. My mom was fat and depressed and always lost games to me (probably trying to build my confidence), which made my young mind see a connection between being fat and losing. When I beat this 13-year-old girl at every game, I told her my theory: "Being fat makes you a loser."

It broke her. I know because that night she stood in the road trying to get hit by a car, shouting, "He's right, I'm a fat loser!"

**I couldn't unlock the secret formula that would make me succeed.**

They sent her home and I never heard what happened as a result of her attempted suicide, and I never told my parents what I said.

When it came to school, and later a career, I knew I was expected to be exceptional, but I couldn't unlock the secret formula that would make me succeed. I also feared success, thinking I didn't deserve it. Thus, I tried to shoot for the middle and lower peoples' expectations of me. I constantly felt like I disappointed my dad. So, to atone for my sins of *not being good enough,*

I sabotaged and punished myself—I also, got fat.

Once it became clear that the school itself was part of the problem, my parents began driving me 45 minutes into town to a private Christian school. All eight grades met in the same room. I enjoyed it more, but they didn't pick up where the other school had left off.

My family eventually moved to a larger town, and I was completely relocated to a new school. Making new friends came much easier than catching up on schoolwork. My parents would move me to two more grade schools seeking a solution before someone finally diagnosed my dyslexia. It was the same year I took an IQ test and scored in the genius range.

For some reason, once my father saw my score on the test, he stopped blaming me for my grades and realized something else had to be going on. Suddenly, the dyslexia diagnosis made it make sense why I never finished or turned in my homework. I'd been memorizing everything they said in class and acing the tests, but with zero credit for homework assignments, my grades sucked. It was too late to get me help with the learning disability; I was just going to have to find a way to be successful in a system not designed for me.

Self-doubt crept in more and more as I became a teen, creating heart wounds and a complicated self-image. We often respond to our wounds by trying to prove them wrong. Sometimes we embrace them. Often, we do both at the same time.

In my case, with women, I became a monster in shining armor. I had caused a vulnerable girl much older than me to try to kill herself. I needed to protect women from the real me. I abandoned working on improving myself and created a "nice guy" shield between myself and other people. They were safe as long as they didn't get to know who I really was. With two older sisters and my mom as the major influences in my life, I idolized women. In trying to protect women from myself, I resented them for being a lot of work, even though it was me and my perception making them a lot of work.

**They were safe as long as they didn't know who I really was.**

By junior college I'd become the original failure-to-launch guy. I kept switching jobs and dated a lot but never long term. I loved learning and spent ten years in junior college looking for something to do other than write books. My dad kept paying for my classes and my car as long as I kept trying to figure out something practical at which to be great.

Throughout college and beyond, I managed to write my first novel on nights, weekends, summers, and holidays. *If nothing else, at least this can be my hobby*, I thought, not wanting to give up the dream. Writing it took sixteen years. I finished it and gave my dad a copy. A friend of his later told me he had read it and loved it. Dad and I never talked about it, though. He died of a heart attack a month after I gave it to him.

Dad's death tore the roof off my world. I stopped sleeping, ate and drank too much—everything I could think of to cope with the pain. I was never going to impress my dad now, even if I someday did figure out the key to success.

About six months later a friend from high school gave me a book called *Wild at Heart*. It completely changed my understanding of Christianity. I'd grown up in a protestant denomination, so I had a good grasp on religion. Yet, no one ever really explained how to have a relationship with God. No one ever told me it was okay to be masculine or that the human condition is brokenheartedness. Suddenly there was hope for redemption, even for the sins I'd knowingly committed.

One night, I had a conversation with God. I was so angry. *How could a God who was good and loving take my father?*

I heard God say, "I took him, and I keep him."

I didn't have a grid for that, so I told him, "You are supposed to be a Father, and I'm not ready to be without a father. If You won't give my father back, I need You to fill in."

God said, "I've been waiting your whole life for you to ask Me to father you. If we do this, you have to be willing to let Me change you."

I said, "If you father me, You can change anything You want."

This interaction changed everything! I wish I could say it was a fast process, and in a way, it was, but it took years to unlearn who I thought I was and to really see myself the way God does.

One of the first lessons I learned was that writing was part of how I process God's creative work in my life. I learned that being faithful to writing is not necessarily connected to making an income. My parents weren't wrong in saying I needed a career for income. I wasn't wrong in believing I needed to write or to be true to myself.

I currently write and publish fiction and non-fiction books and write marketing copy for entrepreneurs, but my favorite writing is the journaling I do with God every morning. That time together has massively accelerated my growth and my productivity toward living a successful life.

Today, I'm totally at peace with my family, having both forgiven and apologized, and they're happy to see me be a better man. I'm a husband and father myself now, so I get to experience what it's like to navigate these situations from the other side of the picture.

> **God healed my wounds and renewed my mind; He also revealed my deep identity.**

God not only healed my wounds and renewed my mind, He also revealed my deep identity. He's shown me the missing secrets I always thought were *out there somewhere*. So, now I coach other creatives in learning to live as a child of a creative God. I'm learning how to line up my talents with God's Kingdom purpose in a way that brings income and advancement.

If you're seeking something elusive, something that makes it all make sense, don't give up. The answer isn't out there, it's inside you. You can take step one right now because it starts with receiving God's grace.

"And Jesus said to them, 'Therefore every scribe who has become a disciple of the kingdom of heaven is like a head of a household, who brings out of his treasure new things and old.'"
—Matthew 13:52 NIV

## Jenny Swart, Author, Artist, Wife, Friend

Jenny lives on the Eastern side of Australia with her husband, Michael. Jenny is a wife and friend, who loves to write and paint.

Jenny went through a long dark season of life where she felt stuck. She felt life was passing her by and that she was captive to the emotional entanglement of destructive events of her past. Eventually resigning from a 30-year career due to burnout and breakdown, she learned to lean into God in order to recover her health.

Prayerfully journaling and painting through those difficult times brought clarity, encouragement, and hope. Having painted prophetically during worship for many years, Jenny learned how to engage with God this way for deeper heart healing.

Having always been quiet and reserved, Jenny feels more at home behind the scenes rather than out in front. She is a compassionate and highly sensitive person who loves to support and encourage others spending many years doing so as part of an art society, on team at an inner-city mission, or as a care support person. She walks with the Lord using the strategies revealed to her over the years and connecting creativity with the Lord through words and art.

Jenny's hope is to inspire creative people, especially women of God who are carrying old wounds, to consider navigating through past pain creatively with God, so they too can be released, unburdened, and untangled as God works with them to be free.

Writing and art by Jenny: **www.wordsnart.com.au**
Learn more about art as self-care at:
**www.artasself-care.com**

# Forgive Yourself and Be Free

On the day I came into the garden of delight, my Beloved stretched His hand out toward me, I took it, and He drew me in close. With a gentle yet confident sweep, He spun me around and we danced together joyfully. As I twirled, I lifted my face in utter delight under the warm clear sky, leaning back into the strength of His arm. *He's got me, I'm safe.* We danced and laughed; it was a heady moment.

Our waltz became a walk side by side, His arm around my shoulders. He led me to the edge of the garden where I saw a passageway hidden in the bushes. As we got closer, I saw what I thought were vines were actually prickly briars. My beloved held me close, and we entered the tunnel of thorns; it was the only way to exit the garden to get somewhere more beautiful and more expansive. Not much light got through that matted, snarly mess, but the light from my Beloved's face shone onto the path directly ahead. I determined to keep close to Him, knowing he would take me from this place of anguish and keep me from getting hurt along the way.

This was part of a dream I had 14 years ago. It came seven months after I began the process of healing my broken heart. I've been walking with Jesus for the past 24 years, along a road that has often been bumpy with twists and turns, ups and downs.

You see, when I was 18, I was raped. When I found out I was pregnant, I was terrified my parents would disown me, so I chose to have an abortion. At that time, it was legal where I lived and quite easy to get. The counseling before the procedure did not offer alternatives nor did it prepare me for the emotional trauma that followed.

Part of me also died that day, and my life was forever changed. A year later, I found myself pregnant again. Since I terminated once, I did it again. Such was my mindset at the time. My low self-worth sank farther, and self-abasement soon kicked in. I couldn't see that it was all connected. Now a shell of a person, I felt lost and numb to deep emotions. I feared God in the wrong way, thinking He was going to punish me for what I had done. So, I chose to hide that part of my past, pushing inexpressible emotions down inside.

Although I looked like I had my act together on the outside, the inside was a whole different story. I was so self-conscious and nervous to the point of mild panic attacks. Perfectionism reigned and I developed mild obsessive-compulsive tendencies. My desire for acceptance was so great I became a chameleon, fitting in with the crowd to please people. I despised myself deeply, not being able to look into my own eyes in a mirror.

> **I despised myself deeply, not being able to look into my own eyes in a mirror.**

Whenever compliments came my way, I couldn't receive them. I would deflect them while thinking *no, not me. If you only knew what I've done, you wouldn't say that.* It was extremely difficult to talk about my abortions, and for years I kept people at arm's length, never allowing anyone to really get to know me. I was so afraid of being rejected.

Before I met Jesus, and even for years after, the aftermath of abortion had been an emotional prison of shame, guilt, and deep sadness—something like walking through an emotional tunnel of thorns which I had been in for more than 20 years.

The shame was like walking around with a gray shawl over my head like it was a safety net. It had the ability to cause me not to see or hear properly, misinterpret, and get offended easily. There was no vibrancy or joy in my life. Shame said *you are not enough and never will be.* It is based on a lie that says *I am a mistake.* It kept me isolated.

The pushed-down feelings started to rise to the surface. Hoping to get my life working a little better, I began three months of counseling. As I dealt with the lies I had believed about myself from childhood, it opened the way to acknowledge and talk for the first time about having been sexually abused; it was also the first time I addressed post-abortion trauma. It was time to tell my mom and dad about being raped and having the abortions, and we were able to clear

180

the air after 27 years of keeping it hidden. They were both very supportive.

As I picked through all my prickly emotions with the counselor, I chose to use art to help get the stuff out of me that was so difficult to talk about. The stuff I couldn't find language for, I painted crudely and abstractly, exorcising the pain through color, shape, and mark making. God revealed to me that my children were boys. I named them and was enabled to draw a portrait of them together. Seeing them, I wept a deeper grief than before. *Would they want to know me after what I have done?* The guilt I carried was so heavy.

Shortly after these counseling sessions, I chose to enter an exhibition of Christian artists and display artwork depicting vulnerable emotions of my journey thus far. I had reached a degree of freedom and it felt so wonderful that I wanted to share it so other women might benefit. I was nowhere near being ready, and doing this was like running ahead of the process I was in. I felt so utterly exposed; it was almost too much to bear. Jesus tells us that putting new wine into old wineskins doesn't work because the old skins break. Trying to live the new life without first updating old thought patterns to new ways of thinking about life broke me. I had not built the emotional capacity to stand in my new truth yet. So, shame engulfed me again.

Many years passed before another aspect of post-abortion pain arose: anger. I was angry, very angry. But I kept it inside because it was not the fault of anyone around me, it was just there, inside me, and at that time I didn't know why. I just wanted to scream to let it all out, but I kept pushing it down inside thinking there was something wrong with me. *I must be weak because I can't seem to get past this pain.*

> **Mostly I was angry at myself, which manifested as self-condemnation.**

I became anxious, critical, and bitter—very prickly indeed. Mostly I was angry at myself which manifested as self-condemnation. Being a quiet, reserved person, the volcano inside wasn't obvious to others. I could not, however, keep the anger totally hidden—it came out passive-aggressively as control. I thought I needed to be in control of everything in my environment, so I wouldn't allow people to do anything for me.

I cycled through moments of ecstatic joy in the presence of the Lord in worship, then having a clouded mind and confusion. I would rally again with faith to trust the course I seemed to be on and relinquishing all to the Lord…before falling back into depression and fatigue. Looking back, I can see the pattern, but it wasn't so obvious while going through it.

Trying to live a good Christian life and help others, I was intricately involved with church life. However, with no personal boundaries in place I ended up getting entangled in complicated people and activities and started losing energy. Unconsciously, what I was really trying to do was atone for my sin. Briars, as it happens, are symbolic of sin. Jesus wore a crown of thorns at the cross which represents carrying away our sins. Even though I heard and read this, I was blinded by my woundedness, unable to forgive myself for what I had done. It's hard to explain, but it was as if I had a voice inside that said things like, *no, abortion is too much to forgive.*

After years of not being able to say *no* to worthy causes and working hard at my job, I began to get sick, experiencing auto-immune disease symptoms and other ailments. It got to the point where I had a breakdown and had to stop working. That was 12 years ago, and I was faced with another prickly dilemma. *Who am I now?*

I didn't realize it until my work was gone, that my identity had been in what I did. There was a certain degree of pride in producing high-quality work efficiently. When I broke down, I slept most of the day, and the pain in my body was such that my strength was 80% diminished. *Who am I if I can't do anything? What value am I if I can't work? What does God think of me now?*

It would have been nice if all the pain left soon after I stopped work, but it didn't. Struggling along with debilitating, poor health felt like pushing through glue. Everything was hard. *Is life supposed to be like this?* I was constantly fatigued where all I could do was sleep. Bloated with Irritable Bowel Syndrome, my brain was foggy and confused, I had no energy to speak and became easily overwhelmed, needing to withdraw from people often for long periods of time. However, I didn't *look* sick.

I had been seeking help from health care professionals for a couple of years before my breakdown. One practitioner told me, "It's like your head is detached from your body. Your body is giving you signals, but you're not listening to it." That comment kick-started research into the body-mind connection and made me think about being spirit, soul (mind, will, and emotions), and body. I needed to consider *all* parts of me.

With another health care professional, after I stopped work, I started reducing stress and implementing personal boundaries while learning more about who I was as a person. *Who am I and what are my preferences?* I was so used to hiding by fitting in with everybody, I didn't know myself. Now, I do. I am a quiet person, very sensitive, and very creative. I pick up feelings and atmospheres around me, not always distinguishing what's mine and what's not. Discovering these things was very helpful, and I finally stopped trying to be someone else and was content learning to be me.

As I began to work on my identity, including taking in what the Bible says about me, my health gradually improved. One of the biggest health breakthroughs came when I stood in front of the bathroom mirror, looked into my own eyes and forgave myself from the heart. I apologized to my soul for not caring for my emotional wellbeing and to my body for not treating it with respect and pushing it too hard. I simply spoke the words that came to mind, knowing God was with me. Something shifted spiritually that day. I used to get extreme fatigue that felt like all my energy got sucked out of my body and mind; all I could do was sleep. I couldn't function, I couldn't even speak, there was no energy left to form sentences. That life-sucking fatigue left that day and has not returned.

For me, healing the wounds of past pain has been a process of many steps. After the breakdown, it took five years for my body to be free from pain but many more for my heart to be mended.

**Healing past wounds has been a process of many steps.**

I began painting as a way to get some enjoyment back into my life. At first, I went overboard. Striving to know everything quickly, perfectionism was still a thing, and I was never satisfied with what I did. I needed to decouple and untangle from the old life and renew, rewire, and learn to live in the new. Healing the deep wounds of my past was like peeling back layers. As I've learned to relax in life, I've relaxed in art, which makes it much more enjoyable.

Remember the dream? That thorny tunnel was dark, but the light of Jesus' face showed the steps directly ahead. As the path before me unfolded, I knew He was always there to give me strength and comfort and courage to face the next aspect of my inner darkness. Even so, there have been times of slowness—some long, some short—according to my willingness to face myself honestly. Walking with God through it all, I have come to know that He is so patient and kind.

A major step forward came five years ago when my mom suggested I read a book containing stories of Christian women who had overcome various life challenges. She told me that one of the stories might be triggering for me. When I read that story of healing from the effects of abortion, I was triggered, but in a good way. It motivated me to find help. In God's infinite love, He guided my steps.

Not being able to find a group to connect with for post-abortion healing, I decided to look on the Rachel's Vineyard website to get hold of a workbook to go through at home and found one. It took me about five months doing a bit every day. My husband was very supportive, and I asked a couple friends for prayer support. On hard days, I would text them and say, "Please pray, it's a difficult section." During this emotionally challenging time, God was so close, and His comfort was tangible. Even while I sobbed, I didn't feel alone. At no time during that process did I feel judged or condemned because that's not God. There is no condemnation in Christ.

During that process, I painted separate portraits of my boys. I also painted them with Jesus in Heaven. Jesus helped me to know they don't hold anything against me and how they long to meet me when I go to them. What a relief to my heart. *They don't hate me.* It was the first time I called myself a mother and the tears flowed—I don't have any other children.

Just after I finished going through the workbook, a prophetic word came to the church I was in. A prophetic word is a message from God to strengthen, encourage, and comfort the church. The word was for women who had experienced abortion, and it said they were totally forgiven in Christ, totally set free by the blood of Jesus. I felt the word was speaking directly to me. I could hardly believe my ears. I sat there stunned; it was surreal. The timing was incredible—you can't make this up!

Through my process, I found that in grieving the loss of a baby, I was also grieving the loss of family and dreams and relationships. The 'what if's' can be tormenting, and the more I allowed sadness to make a home in my heart, the more tormented I felt.

Four years ago, as part of the process from the workbook, I prepared a memorial service and invited my immediate family and a couple of close friends. It was necessary to acknowledge my babies, to grieve their loss in this world, and to say goodbye for now. I'm grateful the Lord showed me that the innocent unborn go

*Michael and Davey grew up in Heaven with Jesus. Painted as I processed through the workbook in 2018.*

straight to Heaven. I used to worry about what happened to them, but now I am assured of where they are. They have grown up in perfection in Heaven.

The dream at the beginning of this chapter had a glorious end to it. That dark, snarly, thorny tunnel stopped at a small cave near the top of a very high cliff—so high, I couldn't see the bottom. From the cave, my Beloved and I looked out over the valley and hills below. Next thing I know, I'm on the back of a huge eagle and we are dipping and diving through the valley then soaring above—a beautiful end to the dream, full of hope for a free future. It was an image I held onto during my healing process. I would often ask the Lord what part of the dream I was walking out at any moment, and He would show me. It helped me stay with it.

About a year after finishing the workbook, which was 11 years after having this dream, I felt I had made it to the cave. Bliss…kind of. The next challenge was overcoming fear of being seen, of being fully known by more than only a few. It was time to start sharing my story.

From the first thoughts of writing my story to finally being able to write this chapter has taken four years. This is a huge step toward freedom, and the timing had to be right. You read earlier what happened when I tried to share my journey before my heart had been prepared. What a bad decision that was. Pushing myself, I was thinking I had to do it, that I had to make something good out of something bad. The more I pushed the more I crumpled. It's not part of my new life's job description to do that. Jesus is the one who restores my soul and flips trauma to bring good purpose from it. I'm finally learning that it's my job to trust and live from a place of rest in Him.

Because I'm a quiet, sensitive person who avoids conflict like the plague, I actually get hives when the threat of vulnerability is looming. I itch, but I don't let it stop me. Whatever I do, I don't stop even if I'm slowed to inching forward, because freedom is found in truth but hiding is staying comfortable in a lie. I've had some stubborn mindset patterns to renew and found degrees of freedom through a variety of heart healing ministries. They work with the soul and spirit, which brings a prosperity of health to the soul—this is life altering and impacts all other areas of life. I'm still a work in progress, but processing has become easier the freer I get.

> **There is no pushing or pulling with Jesus; He sets the pace.**

In Matthew 11:28-30, Jesus said, "Come to Me all you who are weary and burdened, and I will give you rest. Take My yoke upon you and learn from Me, for I am gentle and humble in heart, and you will find rest for your souls. For My yoke is easy, and My burden is light." I learned there is no pushing and pulling with Jesus. He sets the pace. I needed to learn patience as I learned how to care for myself so I could be well. Caring for myself allows me to give care to others.

I started my chapter with a dream because during my most intense healing times, I had a lot of them. I've read how people who have been abused or have trauma in their lives often have disturbing dreams and sleep poorly. This was me, and when I began searching earnestly for wholeness, my dreams were often nightmares, revealing the torment in my soul. I would wake up crying out and feeling afraid. But as my broken heart was mended and my identity was restored, the severity of the bad dreams lessened until I did not feel fear any longer.

When it came, I knew the tunnel of thorns dream was a significant redemptive dream. I wrote it down in detail, asked the Lord what it meant, and waited for the answer. Some understanding came immediately and more came along the way. Insight is a powerful thing to bring hope.

If you identify with this story, then please know that the comfort of God is there for you to draw on as you process through your pain. You can't dismiss your pain because, contrary to popular opinion, time does not heal emotional pain. No matter what age you are, it is never too late to heal. I'm 61 years old now, and my healing journey started only 15 years ago. We are all unique, which means your story will be different from mine, but I offer you mine to give you hope for your future. And yes, you do have a good future because God redeems that which was lost. Healing and change is not easy, but it is possible. I've done it, and it's available for you, too.

> **No matter your age, it's never too late to heal.**

**Angela Yarborough**, author, entrepreneur, outreach minister

As a young mother raising her two daughters, Angela struggled with knowing who God truly was. As a result, she could not model what life in His abundant love looked like. After her little girls became women, Angela was delivered from the pain of her past and began living in His love, peace, and protection. Her heart ached as she watched her daughters walking the same roads, not experiencing the same freedom and life she had found, and looking for answers from the world only God can provide. Knowing she could not go back and do it over again, she began a journey with Him that led her to put her daughters into His hands and trust the promises He had given her for their salvation.

Angela uses her life trials to help other women find freedom in knowing who God is for them and who they are in His eyes. Angela mentors women in prison, rehab, the strip clubs, church, and anywhere else God sends her. As a spiritual mother, she has a passion for all of God's daughters to be free from the lies of the enemy and walk in the beauty God has created them to be.

Later in life, Angela was also given another chance when her third daughter was born. Realizing the importance of a godly mother's role in a daughter's life, she speaks to other moms about this truth and provides them with products to nurture relationships.

To learn more about Angela, purchase her first book entitled *Out of Performance, Into Identity* or browse her creative products for mothers and daughters, including the "LOVE Journal," please visit:

**www.LoveRedeemedMe.com**

188

# CHAPTER NINETEEN
## Angela Yarborough

# Hope for the Prodigals

"I want you to give hope to those mamas out there with prodigal children." This is what God told me to write about in this chapter when I asked Him, and I assumed I knew what that meant.

*Oh, You mean to tell my own restoration story? Got it! Easy peasy!*

Since I had already written an entire book called *Out of Performance, Into Identity* on my story, I would only have to run through and pull out some highlights. *Done.*

But then, He pulled me back and said, "No, I want you to write about your journey as a mom to daughters in need of My restoration."

*Wait a minute, God. That chapter hasn't been finished yet. I am still waiting on You to finish that chapter before I can write about it. I do not have proof of a restored ending to share yet.*

When these words formed in my mind, I realized how easily doubt can creep in and steal our hope. At that moment, I knew exactly why He wanted me to write about the unfinished, broken chapter in my life.

He wants me to tell you how to live in peace, joy, and love while going through the broken chapter of hurting for a child who is lost. He wants me to give you hope that restoration is possible even when it looks like the furthest thing from reality.

Let's start from the beginning, shall we?

"Hey, baby girl!" I said as I answered the phone with anticipation. It was my oldest daughter calling me, which had become a rare occurrence after she reached the ripe old age of 18 and moved out on her own.

"Hey, Mom! I need to talk to you and get something off my chest. I want to tell you before you hear it from anyone else. I'm bi-sexual. I have been for a long time and don't want to hide it any longer."

*Whoa! Okay, I was not expecting that. Stay calm. Think of something motherly to say.*

There was a long pause as I slowly sat down with the phone pressed to my ear. So many thoughts and emotions pulsed through my mind and heart as her words sank in.

*This is not the plan I had for my daughter's future. How did I not know about this major life event? I was not there for her like I should have been as a mother. Why is she telling me all of this over a phone call as if we are discussing dinner plans?*

> **This is not the plan I had for my daughter's future.**

In less than a minute, I experienced the joy of seeing her name pop up on my phone rapidly spiral into anxiety, guilt, fear, and anger. Yet, it seemed like the silence had lasted hours. I was at a loss for words.

*Do I continue to remain silent? Do I cry? Do I ask questions? What do I do? How do I feel? How am I supposed to feel? Which emotion do I address first?*

"Mom, are you still there?" my daughter asked. Knowing I had to say something, I took a long breath.

*Lord, give me Your words.*

As I opened my mouth to speak, words of truth flowed out. "I love you unconditionally. I will always love you, even if we disagree. I will never push you away." Those words were all I could make sense of at this moment. I would need more time to process the rest.

My reassurance of love gave her the open door to pour out her heart to me. Yet for me, the hits kept coming as she told me she no longer believed there was one true God. I reminded her of what the Bible says and was immediately shot down with, "I do not believe in the Bible either. It was a book written by men. It's just another storybook with little meaning for my life." Her closing comment to me will forever be etched in my mind.

"I am in control of my own destiny. I am my own god."

*Who is this child? What have you done with mine? Where has all of this come from? Lord, what do I say? What do I do? I must do something! I have to say something to bring her back to Your truths.*

I wanted to convince her of how wrong she was. I wanted to see her heart and mind line up with what I had discovered in my own

190

journey of finding who God really was and how much He loved her. She had to see all the lies she was buying into. In addition, I wanted it *all* to happen before we ended this heart-wrenching call.

There was another long silence as I wrestled with the fear pulsing through my veins. It felt like she was drowning before my eyes and I couldn't reach her.

*Lord, give me Your words.*

Again, as I opened my mouth to speak, the only words I could form were, "I love you. I hate to hear you no longer believe in God. He is the only constant in life. As your mother, I will not give up on you knowing who He is for you, so I will continue to pray for that. I love you, and I will never turn my back on you."

My heart was incredibly heavy as I hung up the phone that evening. It physically hurt inside of my chest. I wish I could say that shortly after this conversation God supernaturally touched her heart and mind and she is now free from those lies. Unfortunately, I cannot.

> **My heart was incredibly heavy; it physically hurt inside of my chest.**

In fact, one year later, I would have a similar conversation with my second daughter informing me she, too, was also choosing a gay lifestyle over God.

What I can share with you today is my side of the healing journey as a loving mother. Reminding me of the power of love, God has used this journey to show me what true love to others looks like through His eyes, even when we do not see eye to eye with them.

First, I want to push back the curtain and uncover the root of our brokenness. God's Word tells us in the first part of John 10:10, "The thief comes only to steal and kill and destroy..." This thief, aka Satan, is relentless in his pursuit of living up to his job description. He is also a coward and preys on the weak and vulnerable to accomplish this.

Our children are the perfect prey for his lies and destruction—especially our little girls. The enemy knows these little girls have the potential to grow up and be powerful nurturers to the next generation of mothers. These nurturers lead in teaching the next generation about their own personal identity in Christ.

If he can take this power of identity in Christ from our daughters and replace it with lies of false identity, they will only have those same lies to pass down to their daughters. You cannot give something you do not have to give.

I know this all too well, as he tried to destroy my life beginning at the young age of five by taking my innocence through sexual abuse. My long journey of lost identity and taking wrong roads lasted into my mid-adult years.

Yet, praise God, He is the God of restoration and healing and has since brought me through to the other side. That broken chapter has been sealed with His goodness and love. My testimony is being used to give hope to the broken and freedom to the many women who have experienced similar journeys.

Despite the obvious victory obtained through my story, the enemy would continue to throw my past in my face and accuse me. He would try to steal the joy I had discovered.

As a young mother to my two beautiful daughters, I was so broken. I did not have the capacity to give what I did not possess to them as a role model. Day by day, I was trying to survive myself. Although I loved my girls with all my heart, I was not fully present for them as I could have been. I was not able to teach them about a loving God because I, myself, did not know who this loving God was.

The enemy would use this fact to knock me down whenever he could. On the phone that day, he did not miss a chance to remind me of all my failures as a young mother to my daughters.

But God…

This brings us to the second part of John 10:10, where Jesus speaks and promises, "…I have come that you may have life and have it to the full."

A life full and abundant did not mean I sat around in pain, striving to save my daughters. It meant allowing Jehovah-Rapha (the God who heals) to take my pain and use it to grow me closer to Him. Psalm 147:3 tells us, "He heals the brokenhearted and binds up their wounds." Binding up wounds does not always feel good, but He does it from a place of abundant love, and the result leads us to experience more of Him in the most amazing way. His greatest longing is for us to experience a healed heart in relationship with Him.

> **God's great longing is for us to experience a healed heart in relationship with Him.**

Through my own restoration process and falling in love with Jesus, I learned the power of His love. His kind of love will conquer all. As I told my daughters, He is the only constant in life. When all else has fallen around me, His love never fails. He never leaves us to figure it out on our own. Being right there in the pain with us is where He longs to be. While He holds you tight as you walk through the fire together, you will come out on the other side with a better understanding of who you are and who He is for you.

I am going to share a gift that was given to me by God—a gift of communication. He taught me to connect with Him through writing Him *love letters*. Being mostly an internal processor who's always loved journaling, this gift was perfect.

He gave me several frameworks for working through things with Him using these love letters. One of those frameworks is regarding lies. How do you know if what you are hearing is a lie? It will not line up with the fruit of the Spirit from Galatians 5:22-23. If it doesn't speak love, joy, peace, patience, kindness, goodness, faithfulness, gentleness, and self-control, it is a lie—plain and simple.

The framework is based on the word LOVE.

L – Lie. What is the lie or limiting belief I am embracing?

O – Origin. When did I start embracing this lie? Where did it start?

V – Verse. Find a verse of truth in His Word that defeats the lie.

E – Empower. Speak out that truth until it takes root in your heart.

Knowing the accusation of failing as a mother to my daughters was a lie, this was the love-letter framework I chose to talk out the pain I was feeling. I began to ask God when I first started believing it. He brought me back to many memories of when I was a young mother—many memories that still needed His healing touch. There is not enough space here to list them all. However, I will tell you that He doesn't uncover any hurts of the past without walking through them with you and totally restoring them.

The bottom line of the lie stemmed from not forgiving myself. Understanding the idea that He had forgiven me for my past was not enough. I had to acknowledge that when He gave His life on the cross, I was given the gift of freedom and forgiveness of myself. He took my guilt and shame from me as His daughter. If I continued to hold on to my own unforgiveness, I was believing the price He paid was not good enough for me.

*Wow, Lord, I never want to take Your gift for granted.*

Next, I asked Him for a verse from His Word to hold onto as I walk into His truth. In Isaiah 55:11, He promises His Word will not come back to Him void. For this reason, I always look to Scripture to find His promises to stand on as I wait.

The verse He gave me to defeat the lie of unforgiveness, based on guilt and shame I had placed on myself, was Romans 8:1: "Therefore, there is no condemnation for those who are in Christ Jesus."

I took this scripture (promise) He gave me and plastered it everywhere—on my desk, on the fridge, in my car, etc.—so I would see it daily. My mind needed to be renewed with this truth often. *Jesus does not condemn me.* I would speak His promise out loud for my ears to hear. Do you know the verse from Luke 6:45, "...for out of the abundance of the heart the mouth speaks"? I believe it goes both ways. What the mouth speaks will take root and grow in the heart, too. With each day, the roots grew stronger, until one day I realized forgiveness had grown into a full-blown tree of life.

*Okay, God. But what about my girls? What am I going to do about them? They need your truth and help.*

"You, baby girl, are going to place OUR girls into My loving and capable hands. I will do the rest."

*Yeah, I know You love them, Lord, but I need to do something. I cannot stand by and watch while they drift away.*

"Do you trust Me?"

I wanted to say *yes*, but I could not get past the reality of what I

194

saw with my own eyes and heard with my own ears every time I was around my daughters. Looking through my eyes, I could not see any heart change taking place in either one of them.

"Trust in the LORD with all your heart and lean not on your own understanding; in all your ways submit to Him, and He will make your paths straight" from Proverbs 3:5-6 would become my promise to stand on during this season of waiting.

Knowing this was a test of my heart toward Him, I agreed to place them into His hands.

Most days were a struggle, attempting to take them back from His capable hands and try to "fix" their hearts with my own strength. Yet, He was so patient and loving to remind me of His love for them—far deeper than anything I could imagine or replicate. *He is trustworthy; He will love them enough to restore life back into them.* After all, He's their Creator. As He was forming them inside my womb and breathing life into them, He had a great plan for their lives. That plan has not changed. He has not changed.

Psalm 138:8 would be another promise for this season. The Lord would fulfill His purpose in my daughters (His daughters). His steadfast love would endure forever. He would not forsake the work of His hands in our daughters.

**His plan has not changed. He has not changed.**

Eventually, as this truth took root in my heart, He began to speak to me about seeing my daughters through His eyes. This began a journey of healing I never saw coming.

A while back, I was invited to speak to a group of women in the prison system and give my testimony of restoration. As I spoke for the first time in public about my own personal brokenness, I looked out at the women and saw tears flowing down their faces. My heart broke as He spoke to me at that moment: "I am giving you these spiritual daughters to shepherd and love. You are an amazing mom, and as you pour life and hope into these daughters I am trusting you with, so will I be pouring life and hope into your daughters that you have trusted Me with."

By the end of my testimony, we were all crying.

Since that day, He has broadened my spiritual daughters to include those from prostitution, the strip clubs, and those rescued from sex trafficking. I am incredibly humbled that He would choose me to be a spiritual mother to His beautiful prodigal daughters. I meet with most of my daughters weekly and love them with all my heart.

Love is the answer, my friend. When we can lay down our own understanding and our own biases and quit looking through our human lenses and look through God's eyes of love, that's when things will change. In the beginning, I thought my purpose was only to give hope to the broken-hearted women who I served. However, as He has allowed me to see the worst-case scenarios come to His light and love, I realize how much I need them, too, to keep my hope and trust aflame. We all need each other.

> **We all need each other!**

Lastly, yet surely not least, He has given me scriptures to pray over my girls daily. Some of these scriptures have been words of encouragement spoken to me by friends, some have come through books I have read, and others have been given directly by God while reading the Word or in dreams. His words give me comfort, as I know He keeps all His promises to us.

Being the God of abundant love, last year He blessed me with a gift in the form of a prophetic dream—He speaks to me often through dreams. In this dream, I was in a praise and worship service with my hands lifted to Him. As I opened my eyes and looked to my right, I saw one of my daughters standing beside me with her hands raised high in praise, singing words of love and surrender to Him. What I felt in that dream cannot be easily described. If I'm ever tempted to doubt what I see in the physical realm, I close my eyes and hold on to the feeling He allowed me to feel that night. In my heart I know I will feel it again, but next time it won't be just a dream; it will be in physical form. One day soon, both of my daughters will stand beside me and give praise to the God of their salvation.

God is not a respecter of persons. What He does for one, He will do for another. Our testimonies, like the ones you are reading in this book of our broken chapters, are invitations for you to grab ahold of that same hope and know He will do it for you, too.

**Eileen Noyes**, author, speaker, coach

Eileen Noyes is fully stepping into the next phase of her calling as an author, speaker, and founder of Lady Bellator—coaching and mentorship for high-profile women. In her book *Sidelined No More*, Eileen details her own journey of high-profile living in the NFL world, where she slowly shriveled into an empty shell of outward beauty. She went from having a model family and being the trophy wife who seemed to have it all together, to having everything come crashing down for all eyes to see. God helped her pick up the pieces of a broken marriage, endure single motherhood to her eight children, and gain strength to remarry and start all over. Now she desires to share her story and help women navigate their own journeys. Her passion is to help women in high-profile relationships—such as pro-sports—to find themselves again, not cave into someone else's mold or expectations, and find a safe outlet of wisdom, understanding, resources, and coaching to deal with all the areas of life that come with living life in the public eye.

Author Eileen Noyes resides in California with her husband Michael and eight of their 15 combined children. She's a stay-home mom turned entrepreneur who juggles family life, fitness, fun, and business. She loves being a strength training boy-mom to her seven growing boys and enjoys the girly, creative hobbies with her one and only mini-me.

For more information on Eileen as a speaker or for coaching please contact **hello@ladybellator.com or visit:**

**www.LadyBellator.com**

## CHAPTER TWENTY
## Eileen Noyes

# God's Voice of Truth

I was told I wasn't created in the image of God because I was a woman.

I was told God didn't hear my prayers because I wasn't created in His image.

I was told I could not go to heaven because of my ethnicity.

I was told my value was contingent on my obedience to my husband.

I was told I had a Jezebel spirit because I wore make-up and didn't cover my hair.

I was told I was the enemy of my home.

I was told I had nothing more to offer if I couldn't bear any more children.

These words were spoken to me after 15 years of marriage and birthing seven beautiful children. These words were spoken to me by a man I loved and knew for close to half my life. These words were spoken by someone I respected and whose zeal for God was what I admired most.

It all began with one comment, one spoken sentence that rocked my foundation to its core: "You know you're not created in the image of God, right?"

That was a question (more of a statement) posed to me one morning as I was getting ready for the day. I remember brushing my teeth while processing what I just heard. Shocked at his statement, I spewed out the toothpaste that filled my mouth. "What did you say?" Assuming he was joking, I waited for the punchline, but it never came. In total seriousness, he attempted to reason with me on how he came to that conclusion and was fully convinced of his position. He tried to persuade me of the same.

To me, being in God's image was a given, a no-brainer, Biblical

Truth 101. "So God created man in His own image; He created him in the image of God; He created them male and female." Genesis 1:27 says this.

Somehow he explained away what was in plain sight and continued with his thought process. As he went on, all sorts of thoughts began racing through my head. *So where does that leave me? Am I somewhere in between man and animal? How am I seen by God? Can I pray to God like a man does? How can I abide in Him if He did not create me in His image? How can I be a daughter of God if I'm not like Him? Did Jesus die for me or for the male gender only? Does that make our kids half image of God and half not? Is man supposed to be fruitful and multiply with another man?* I probably voiced a dozen more questions as I felt my blood pressure rise.

I can't recall his response or if I was even paying attention to anything he said at that point. But I remember saying, "If this is true, this changes everything for me. If this is true, then who am I to God?" I cautioned him, "This is foundational truth. If Satan can get you to believe that lie, then he can have a field day on anything else in the Bible."

With the morning totally thrown off by this conversation, he left me with his attempt of consolation. "Eileen, it's not a big deal. This really doesn't change anything anyway." Yet, in the days and weeks that followed, what initially was "not a big deal" became a monster increasingly rearing its ugly head. I saw a change in his demeanor toward me as he brought up more discussions of men and women not being equal. I saw the partnership of two people who built a life together—two opposites who complemented each other, two voices that encouraged and challenged each other—vanish before my eyes.

As time passed, he talked more and more of woman being created *for* man, forbade me to listen to certain pastors, discouraged the family from listening to women preach from the pulpit, and taught our kids to refute any teaching from their Christian school about women being created in the image of God.

As we held our family Bible studies where we both normally interacted with the kids and where we both had input of our thoughts and perspectives, my role was reduced to preparing material that came with the study, dictating his teaching on the white board, and tending to the littlest one to keep her occupied—all while remaining silent.

In order to avoid the fighting in front of the kids, to keep the peace in our home, and to dodge criticism or rebuke from my spouse, my voice faded to nothing. The more he consumed himself with his new teaching, the more my foundation was being shaken, and the more I second guessed what I believed. All those questions I asked in sarcasm and with the thought of total absurdity during our initial discussion turned into real doubts plaguing my every thought.

> **My identity—my prized possession and my anchor— was the thing I began to question.**

My identity, what I knew to be my most prized possession and my anchor since the day I decided to give my life to Jesus, became the very thing I began to question. The most secure relationship I'd ever known became the one I was losing sight of. Not only did I feel a wedge between my husband and myself, but now I felt a wedge between me and the One who I had always known as my Abba Father.

"Lord, how do I do this? How is this not a big deal? Who am I, and do You even hear me? All those precious promises in Your Word, do they even pertain to me?"

To not know who I was in the grand scheme of things felt like I was just a blob who took up space in this world. That one initial statement voiced from someone I loved—the concept that wasn't supposed to be a big deal—had me questioning my identity, my relevance, and my significance as a wife, a mother, and a child of God (if that was even the case).

That was Satan's plan: to use one lie to cause confusion and doubt—one lie to open the door for more and more deception. It was one lie to target my foundation, shaking the solid ground on which everything else in my life was established. It was the scheme of the devil used to trip me up, and unfortunately it was working.

After months and months of arguing, trying to give logical reasons to refute his thinking, and after attempting to give him Scripture to back up my beliefs, nothing sufficed. I gave up trying. I was weary and had no fight in me. That place, however, was where I needed to be—to stop fighting my own battles and let God be my defense.

During my Bible reading one morning, I came across the scripture from 2 Corinthians 3:18 (ESV): "And we all, with unveiled face, beholding the glory of the Lord, are being transformed into the same image from one degree of glory to another. For this comes from the Lord who is the Spirit."

I had read this scripture many times before, but this time it hit me in a whole new way. God knew exactly what I needed to hear; He knew this scripture would hit on every point. We ALL are beholding the glory of God. We ALL are being transformed into His very IMAGE, which is the essence of who God is, the representation of His character, bearing the righteousness and holiness of God. This transformation comes from the Lord who is the SPIRIT, which is the *nonphysical* part of a person and having no reference to body or gender—no male, no female, no ethnicity.

For me, hearing this scripture at that moment was a mic drop. It settled everything in my own spirit and gave me the peace and assurance I needed. I was confident once again that I *was* created in His image, I *was* His daughter, He *did* hear my prayers, and I wasn't a blob in this world just existing. My relationship with God (Father, Jesus, and Holy Spirit) proved faithful to pull me from the dark pit I was in.

I had no idea how much I needed this reassurance. In this season, I didn't realize how crucial this revelation was. I didn't yet know how vital it would be that I heard the voice of God over the voice of the enemy...

This one lie my husband believed—the same lie the devil tried to use to trip me up—opened the door to a world I never would have imagined. This belief birthed a path so different than the one I walked, so different from the experience of God's love, grace, and mercy, and so different from the Jesus I knew. This path led my husband to involvement with a Black Hebrew Israelite teaching contrary to the biblical teachings we had followed throughout our marriage.

Our family was now required to follow the Old Testament Law. My kids and I were deemed as *property*. Head covers were required for me and my daughter. Having multiple wives was the norm and was the intended plan soon to be implemented. The temperament of our home was contingent on my obedience to my spouse.

The man, husband and father, the head of our home was the one who was supposed to lead us, protect us, and reflect the Father's love to us. All of that slowly disappeared from our family because truth was replaced with a lie.

> **Seeing someone you love and respect become almost unrecognizable is a difficult experience.**

Seeing someone you love and respect become almost unrecognizable in every way is a difficult experience. It was so hard to see someone so vocal about Jesus evolve into someone so far off from God's message of hope. How heartbreaking it was to experience the truth of God's Word turn into something so twisted, perverted, and full of deception.

Seeing this drastic change come over the man who was to lead us not only tore me apart, it made me realize the devil was going after the rest of us as well. Mark 3:27 speaks of this: "First tie up the strong man, then you can plunder everything in his house."

At that point I had to be the one to stand in the gap for my family and be a voice of truth to cut through the cloud of lies in our home. It meant having to stay continuously close and connected to God so my kids and I wouldn't fall for the same deception. It meant contending for my family in prayer, being filled with the truth of God's Word, and abiding in the Holy Spirit for direction on my every step. *Lord, help me do all this while holding it emotionally together.*

It was crucial for me to hear and know God's voice to help me navigate this confusing time. I had to hear His voice above all else to keep me from doubt, discouragement, bitterness, and confusion that wanted so badly to consume me and the rest of our family.

"You will keep in perfect and constant peace the one whose mind is steadfast and stayed on you, because he trusts and takes refuge in

You." This verse from Isaiah 26:3 was everything to me. It was my anchor when I doubted, when I was discouraged, and when I was tempted to give up. There were times the devil tried to use my husband to tell me I was rebellious, not submissive, not good enough, "not perfect like God is perfect," and that I had nothing to offer anymore after having two miscarriages. It was during these moments when my trust in God and my mind totally focused on Him brought me back to truth: *God's Word is louder than all the lies.*

This perfect-peace verse carried me through one of the hardest trials I've ever gone through. His peace held me through all the turmoil as my husband pursued cult involvement. My mind was stayed on God when the children and I had to step away from the deception and toxicity of that teaching. My trust was in Him even as divorce came into the picture. My refuge was in Him with all the uncertainty that followed.

I had to train myself to hear His voice over all the noise I was hearing when this took place; the noise of judgment from the outside world who didn't understand what was going on in our home, the noise of speculation that I was crazy and unstable, and the noise of well-intended counsel of the church to go back home when my kids and I stepped away from the toxic and dangerous situation. *So much noise.* So many voices wanted to drown out God's voice, but thankfully it didn't work anymore.

> **I had to train myself to hear His voice over all the noise.**

God equipped me, strengthened me, and prepared me for the battles ahead. I had to immerse myself in the Word of God as my sword to fight the devil's schemes. When I understood God's truth about who He was, who I was, and who my real enemy was, then I could fight the *right* battles. I had to be so filled with what God said that His voice came out through mine.

The voice the devil was desperately trying to silence—my voice that was quieted and weary for so long—finally started to take a stand. No longer could I remain silent as the devil attempted to devour our home. As his plan was to take down the rest of the family, God's plan was to put the devil in his place, to use his evil for our good, to deliver us from the snares of the one who thought he had us, and to use my voice with His to execute this plan. My voice aligned with His is powerful.

My once timid and weary voice turned into the one now strong and firm in prayer for my family.

My voice spoke the truth of God's Word out loud to combat the confusion and the lies the enemy tried to bring into our home.

My voice spoke of God's love to my children, assuring them this wasn't their fault, reminding them of His love, praying His peace over them during the storms, and pointing to His goodness and faithfulness even in the hardest of trials.

My voice spoke declarations of God's promises to us. He promises to never leave us nor forsake us (Deuteronomy 31:8). He promises to protect us, strengthen us, and hold us with His righteous right hand (Isaiah 41:10). He promises to renew our strength as we wait on Him (Isaiah 40:31). He promises to be our defense (Exodus 15:2-3). He also promises to work all things out for our good when we love Him (Romans 8:28).

My voice spoke blessings over the ones who cursed me so that I can put the devil to shame.

My voice spoke forgiveness over my ex-husband to break any chain of bitterness trying to take root in my heart.

My voice spoke praises to God in all the circumstances that came our way.

My voice spoke in the authority of Jesus to rebuke the devil and bind his schemes and his attempts to take more than he already had.

My voice spoke thanks and gratitude for getting us through, protecting me and the children, and for restoring the joy in us as we moved forward from that long season.

As hard as it was, I know the effects of this rewritten chapter will impact generations to come for His glory. God has reassured me of how faithful He is to those whose hearts are loyal to Him, how compassionate He is to those who cry out to Him, and how strong I am in Him when my heart fully trusts in Him.

> **I realized how much the devil wanted to silence my voice. Can you relate?**

I realized how much the devil wanted to silence my voice. Can you relate? He tried tirelessly to make me believe my voice didn't matter, even trying to deceive me to believe that I had nothing to say. No longer will I fall for this lie! It's God's voice of truth that I cling to. Over all others, it's His voice I want to hear. His voice gives strength to mine.

With all I went through, my passion is to give a message of hope and encouragement to those who need it. Maybe you feel stuck in a silent place; a place where lies want to take over. My desire is to comfort those in affliction in the same way He comforted me in mine. My purpose is to come alongside other women whose voices have been silenced, who have lost sight of who they are, and who need a voice of truth. They must know they are not the lies they have been told.

My God, my Father, the One who cannot lie, tells us this (you can speak these over yourself):

I am created in the image of God.

I am His daughter whom He loves and invites to come to His throne of grace.

I am covered by the blood of Jesus and my salvation rests in Him alone.

I am precious in His sight and I'm fearfully and wonderfully made.

I am a friend of God.

I am His workmanship created in Christ Jesus to do good works.

I have much more to offer than just the blessing and honor of bearing children.

In His goodness and in His sense of humor, even though my value didn't come from having children, I didn't realize I was pregnant with my eighth child during the thick of our storm. It was as if God made lemonade when life tried to throw me lemons. It was my joy that came in the morning. Not only did my voice speak blessings to my seven children, my voice spoke life, truth, praise, thanksgiving, and protection over this new little one as well.

How good and faithful our God is, taking what the devil meant for evil—the broken chapters of our lives—and making them a beautiful story of redemption.

**" How good and faithful our God is! "**

## Krista Dunk, author, publisher, worshipper

Krista Dunk is an author, speaker, the project director for 100X Publishing, and founder of the Author Acceleration Academy. A teacher at heart, Krista has written eleven books so far. Her first book, *Step Out and Take Your Place*, was published in early 2011. Along with her first book and its companion journal and workbook, she has also published a devotional, the *Ninja Kitty* children's book series, the *Ideas and Strategies Journal*, a book for aspiring authors called *Author Acceleration*, as well as books in *The Abundance Plan* book series.

As a child and young adult who struggled with timidity, Krista now finds herself speaking and training in front of audiences large and small. She is passionate about helping people get a vision for how their life could look and to step out into it. Working with authors since 2012 has been one of Krista's greatest joys.

Krista and Chris, her husband of 30 years, live in Washington State and have two amazing young-adult children, Christian and Karissa, and a green-eyed cat named Lovie.

Learn more at:

**www.KristaDunk.com**
**www.AuthorAccelerationAcademy.com**

## CHAPTER TWENTY-ONE
### Krista Dunk

# The Dream Lives

"Fetal demise" was what the radiologist said in her side office after the ultrasound. Stunned, my mind had a hard time processing those words. My mother clasped her hand over her mouth, and I sat silently staring at the doctor's face. After an explanation of some technicalities and trying to help me gain understanding as to what happened, I quietly gained the understanding of *there is no heartbeat; your baby died*.

"Do you have any more questions?" she asked.

Voice shaking, I said, "Can I see the ultrasound pictures?" Somehow seeing those images would at least prove our baby's existence. I had to see it with my own eyes. At 12 weeks along in our very first pregnancy, this was not the news I was expecting to hear at this appointment. My husband, Chris, was on a business trip, so my mother had come with me to the ultrasound appointment. The due date would have been on her birthday.

Not knowing what to say, my mother and I trudged to the parking lot. Her tears came as we got to my car. Mine came later, and especially when I had to call Chris to let him know what happened. How do you have a conversation like this over the phone? How do you tell your spouse this kind of news? And what did they mean when they said there was "evidence of a second one" as the radiologist and ultrasound technician were talking? Was it possibly twins?

Earlier this same week, our good friends who had a newborn daughter experienced a tragedy. Their two-month-old suddenly died from a birth defect in her heart that had gone undetected. They were devastated, and we were heartbroken for them. Their daughter's funeral was two days later. Loss piled upon loss. After the funeral, we told them our news, and more tears came.

I was scheduled for a D&C procedure several days later. The same afternoon of my D&C, the four of us left for an eight-day road trip.

For most of that first evening, I laid down in the third-row seat of the minivan, in physical and emotional pain, trying to come to terms with what had just happened. Our friends needed to get away from their home with an empty nursery, and Chris and I had the following week off without any travel plans—it was unusual for us to have time off without a trip planned. God knew.

**"Loss piled upon loss."**

In planning for my ideal life, I'd always thought *gee, 27 seems like the perfect age to become a mother.* We had been married seven years by then and started out our marriage with a *someday* attitude about having children. Finally agreeing it was time, this result was painful. It was also painful for our parents. This would have been their first grandchild.

Waves of loss came over the next days, weeks, and months. The sting of having conversations with people who knew we had been expecting came for a while—family first, then coworkers, friends, and others. As more and more women found out, I was surprised to learn how common miscarriage is. Several women revealed they'd experienced it, too.

At first it seemed appropriate to let the grief show and to talk about it, but as months passed, the loss was internalized. Who would this person have been? What would they have become? It was the loss of a hoped-for child, the loss of a dream, and the feeling of failure, wondering if the miscarriage was somehow my fault. *What could I have done differently?*

I remember one night not being able to fall asleep, quietly crying and praying, the stress unbearable. Lying in bed, as I cried out to God, I felt a tangible embrace. Nothing like this had ever happened to me before. Suddenly, the spiritual realm we cannot see became a reality. With the embrace, all the anxiety and pain melted away in a moment, replaced by a warm comfort I cannot fully explain. Jesus must have given me a hug, and I desperately needed it.

There was another time on a lunch break at work when I was in my car, crying. I called my sister at her office. Pouring out all of my fears and concerns, she was a source of encouragement and a caring listening ear. I know she was praying for us.

During this time, I sought the Lord more than I ever had before. Mostly I was looking for answers, hope, help. My relationship with Him deepened, and a new trust started forming. There was even a time shortly after when a family member was having a difficult time getting pregnant, and I gave them a prophetic word. Sitting on softball bleachers while watching a game, she explained how in-vitro fertilization and other fertility treatments hadn't worked. They were looking for sperm donors and whatever else might result in a pregnancy. She was feeling desperate. In that moment, I just knew something. I said, "No, you won't need to do any of those things. It's going to be Mike. It will work."

> **I was looking for answers, hope, help.**

She was skeptical, but we talked about it for a few more minutes, then went on to other topics. About two months later, she called me after taking a pregnancy test. "You're never going to believe this. You said it, and it's true—I'm pregnant!" Only God could have given me this information and faith. I was so happy for them! But still sad for us.

Reading my Bible one day, I had a thought. *God has promises for children, right? If He has promises about giving us children and that children are a blessing from Him, I'm going to find all the promises and pray them for us. I will remind Him what He has said and stand on those promises.* I scoured the Bible for any and all verses that mentioned children being a blessing from the Lord—verses like Psalm 127:3-5, Psalm 113:9, and Isaiah 54:13. I read them. I said them. My husband and I discussed them. These verses formed a rock in my spirit that could not be moved. God would bless us with children. He had to. He promised.

With each month passing and not being pregnant, it was still a source of frustration. And my husband's work travel schedule didn't make it any easier! Being gone on strategic weeks was, of course, problematic…

When the baby's due date came and went six months later, something, someone, was missing.

Around the same time frame, I switched jobs—going from

working in a state office as an HR admin to working as a sign language interpreter at a local high school. It felt like a risk to make this transition, but one I had been working toward for several years. It was time. And it kept my mind focused on a new season rather than the season of loss. Two months after that, I took a pregnancy test on a Sunday morning. Positive! I put the test stick in my purse and showed it to my mother at church. Our eyes welled up. Chris called his mother that day to give her the good news. She was ecstatic.

Even though the rock of faith had been built, I was excited but cautious. I was nervous, happy, fearful, confident, a little bit sick, and everything all rolled up into one. This child's due date would be in November. At that point, I didn't care if the due date was Christmas Day as long as the pregnancy went well and the baby was healthy. With every appointment, we prayed all was going well, and it was.

At 18 weeks along, we had the first ultrasound. What an amazing day that was! Chris was so excited—the look on his face was precious as we saw our baby actively moving around. I remember the technician saying, "We can't always tell the sex of the baby, but...oh, wait, I *can* tell. Do you want to know?" Yes, we did. There he was, our son.

I wondered if it was going to be a boy. Several years prior, I'd had a dream in the night. This dream seemed so real and unusual. In this dream, I was upstairs in my childhood home (where my mother and step-father still lived at the time). Sitting on the floor, I had a baby girl in my arms, my daughter, and a very young boy, my son, was across the room. My young son was worried, saying, "Mommy, what is this? What are we doing?" like he wasn't sure what was happening. I told him, "It's okay, don't worry. We're just here." And that's all I remember.

**This dream seemed so real and unusual.**

As the pregnancy progressed, I made it through the strange cravings for Cheetos and bananas, the hot summer days, and having his little head jammed into my ribs. He was breech, and at some point the doctor was concerned. "We need to do a procedure where we manually try to turn him head down before he gets too big." This was at about 34 weeks along. We scheduled the procedure for the following week—at 35 weeks. Little did they know that I had a defect in my uterus that would have made turning him impossible.

On the Wednesday of the next week, in the wee hours of the morning, I woke up feeling a small rush of fluid. Honestly, I thought the baby had kicked me and I peed a bit. But somehow it felt different. I got up, went to the bathroom, then went back to bed. That morning, I got to the high school for work at 7:30. Between every single class period that morning, I was in the bathroom. Mind you, that's not necessarily out of the ordinary for a woman who's 35 weeks pregnant, but the frequency seemed odd.

At a late-morning break, I talked to one of my coworkers who had three children. "So…how do you know if your water broke?" I figured she would know.

Her eyes got serious. "What?"

"I feel like I have to go to the bathroom all the time today. And I felt something strange in the middle of the night. I'm sure it's nothing."

"You need to go and have it checked soon. Right now."

"Really? He's not due for five weeks, and I'm sure it's nothing. I'm fine."

She insisted I call my doctor's office. I heeded her advice, and they wanted me to come in, just in case. Their office was only six minutes from the high school. So, I went. I even told the vice principal I'd be back after lunch. Nope.

After the doctor checked, they did find amniotic fluid and I was dilated to three centimeters. "We need you to go over to the hospital right now for a C-section. They will be expecting you."

*Oh no, Chris is hours away at a work meeting.* My call to him started out, "Hi, where are you now?" He and a coworker sped back to town as fast as they could.

Christian Michael was born with the umbilical cord wrapped around his neck three times and wasn't breathing. The first noise we heard from him was a series of sneezes, then a cry. During the time after the C-section when they stitch you up, the doctor gave me the first news about some abnormalities in my body. "You only have one ovary that works and no fallopian tube at all on the bad ovary's side." *Well, no wonder it takes a while to get pregnant.*

Being a preemie, they allowed Christian to stay in our hospital room intermittently, going between there and the "special care nursery." The next day, however, he had to take up residence in the nursery—he had developed jaundice. Along with jaundice, he wasn't able to nurse well yet, they detected a heart murmur, they suspected he had hip dysplasia, his little nose was squished to one side, and one of his toes partially overlapped another.

Through all of those things, I experienced the peace that surpasses all understanding as it says in Philippians 4:7. "He's going to be just fine," was my reply to any concerning news. And he was. By the time he left the hospital's special care nursery unit just 12 days later, his jaundice and heart murmur were gone. A few weeks later, it was confirmed that his hip sockets were fine, too. Eventually, his nose and toes looked perfect. By the time he was eight months old, you'd never know he was a preemie.

> **Through all of those things, I experienced the peace that surpasses all understanding.**

Fast forward a couple years, we decided to try for another child. About six months later, I was pregnant. Per my dream, I suspected this baby would be a girl. When I asked two-year-old Christian if he thought he was going to have a baby sister or a baby brother, he answered, "It's going to be a baby sister." He was right!

At the ultrasound, there she was, little sister. While pregnant with her, I remember how she would be still most of the night, but as soon as the first voices spoke in the morning, she was immediately active and alert. She was due in December. In September, we were in the middle of building a new house. We put the house we had been living in up for sale, and it sold in one day. So, technically, we were homeless! We moved into my mother and step-father's large house, taking over the upstairs area.

One October day, just after he turned three, Christian had a preschool pumpkin patch trip. Moving his booster seat into our truck, I felt the familiar small rush of fluid and had a sinking feeling. *I am only 32 weeks pregnant; this can't be happening again.* We went on the field trip, and later that day, Christian and I went out to an early dinner with my mom and sister. I hadn't felt more fluid leaking, but I did start to feel crampy. After confessing my suspicion to them, off I went to the hospital. My mother took Christian home, and my sister accompanied me. It was confirmed—I was in labor again and my water had a slow leak.

This time, doctors were worried about the baby's lungs. "At 32 weeks, they may not be developed enough yet. We need to stop your labor for as long as possible and give her more time." This was easier said than done. On top of that, they would not allow her to be born at this hospital—the hospital in our town—at this early stage. They did not have the advanced neonatal equipment in case she needed it. I was sent by ambulance to a larger hospital 40 minutes away, where I spent four days laying in a bed, trying not to move, and being given shots to mature her lungs. Chris was splitting his time at home with Christian, working on a couple projects at the new house that had to be completed, and with me at the hospital. The baby was head down, so they were going to allow me to deliver her naturally, especially since she was going to be small.

After four days, I was sick as a dog because of the shots and the baby started showing signs of distress. She was lethargic and not responding to stimuli.

"You need a C-section as soon as possible. You will not be able to have a natural birth. It can't wait."

Chris made it to the hospital just in time, and this time my sister was able to come into the C-section room, too. The doctor asked what the baby's name would be, and we said, "Karissa." As they worked to remove her, she started crying before she was even out which they said was very unusual. "It's a girl" was confirmed, and I remember my husband crying and saying, "She's still a girl!" which makes me smile even now. They whisked her away to the NIC unit, and he followed. My sister stayed with me as they worked to finish up.

After the C-section, this doctor gave me the second bit of news about my fertility issues. "You only have half a uterus. Every baby you'll ever have will be a preemie. They'll get to a certain size and not fit anymore." That's when we decided two healthy children, a boy and a girl, was enough.

She also gave me another diagnosis: necrotic fat scar tissue, most likely from the previous C-section, had formed in my abdomen and was looped around some of my intestines. Eventually, it would have pinched them off, which could potentially lead to death. She performed a surgical procedure to remove it, then stitched everything back up. Recovery for me this time was difficult.

Karissa Promise looked like a little doll with velvety hair. According to the NIC unit nurses, they had never seen a baby born at 32 weeks with absolutely nothing wrong with them. She never even had jaundice. She was just small, so she had to stay in the hospital for 17 days until she gained a little weight.

Looking back on all of this, I can see God's hand working in so many ways, in so many details. From dreams, to a week's leave from work with no plan to go anywhere. Not trying to turn my son while in the womb, and all of his post-birth issues being resolved. Then the second C-section process, catching my intestinal problem, Karissa's surprise perfection, and more. And had that first pregnancy been twins, they wouldn't have made it. God worked it all out—every little piece.

A couple months later, it hit me—I was sitting in the upstairs room of my childhood home with a baby girl in my arms and a young son. We lived there until Karissa was five months old and our new house was completed. The dream became reality.

Despite my body's abnormalities and our broken hearts because of the loss of our first baby, there was still hope. With trust in God and His plan, I believe we should continue to hope for good to come even after disappointments, loss, and experiencing things we may not understand.

Today, my children are 21 and 18. We are so thankful for them, and I carry this story in my heart as a testimony of a great work God has done. When we look closely, we can spot God at work in our life's story—in big shifts and tiny details.

As a final note, after a conference three years ago, I was talking with a friend named Magnus who is a prophet. He asked about my children, and I told him about Christian and Karissa. He started prophesying about my family and two kids, sharing what he saw God saying. He paused and then said, "Was there a third?" It hit my heart hard, as it still sometimes does. "Yes, there was a baby that we lost."

> **When we look closely, we can spot God at work in our life's story—in big shifts and tiny details.**

My mouth dropped when he said, "It's a daughter," and he went on to explain how she's with the Lord and prays for our family and can't wait to see us. Even as I type this, it brings up deep emotions. When I got home, I told my husband and kids about this. Karissa decided her sister needed a name and gave her one. So, her name is Karrah. Karrah, we can't wait to see you either, and we know you are safe in His arms until then.

"Hope deferred makes the heart sick, but when desire is fulfilled,
it is a tree of life." —Proverbs 13:12

# Prayer

Salvation Prayer:

*God, I want to know You more and know Your great love for me. Please forgive me—I am sorry for my sins. There have been many, and the Bible says You sent Jesus to die and pay the price for my sins. I believe that Jesus is Lord and Savior, and I want Him to come into my life and lead me. Thank you, God, for the help, forgiveness, joy, and new life You freely give to me! I receive it all. In Jesus' name, amen.*

Prayer for Strength and Courage:

*God, You are the Lion of Judah, the King of Kings. You know my inmost being, my heart, and my life's calling. You call me blessed, a chosen generation, an overcomer, set apart for Your purposes. Lead me in the everlasting way and help me to trust Your faithfulness and limitless power. Give me the strength I need each day to do all the things You've called me to do. I am strong in You and in Your mighty power. In Jesus' name, amen.*

Prayer for God's Help:

*God, You are good and I know You love me. You have good plans for me and good thoughts toward me. In my Broken Chapters, please come with Your eternal pen and rewrite every piece for Your glory, for Your Kingdom purposes, and for my good. I give you permission to have Your way in every area of my life. Help me to steward my relationships, work, money, health, material things, and opportunities well. Please cover my life and family in the blood of Jesus for protection, cleansing, and empowering. Hide me in the shadow of Your wings, I pray. In Jesus' name, amen.*

Thank you for reading! We pray these stories were impactful, encouraged you, and ignited your faith to believe God is willing and able to help you in every area of your life.

To connect more with this book's authors individually, please see the information supplied on their chapter's bio page.

Join our reader community on Facebook now in our **Broken Chapters – fans and faith** group

If you enjoyed this book, please visit Amazon.com and Goodreads.com to leave a positive review for *Broken Chapters*.
and
consider purchasing a copy of this book to encourage a friend.

Exclusive Publishing for Kingdom Entrepreneurs

100XPublishing.com

www.ingramcontent.com/pod-product-compliance
Lightning Source LLC
Chambersburg PA
CBHW071425090426
42737CB00011B/1567